RETREAT FROM POWER

VOLUME TWO
After 1939

RETREAT FROM POWER

Studies in
Britain's Foreign Policy
of the
Twentieth Century

VOLUME TWO
After 1939

Edited by
DAVID DILKS
Professor of International History
University of Leeds

© David Dilks, Sarvepalli Gopal, Margaret Gowing,
Graham Ross, Edward Spiers, Colin Strang 1981

First published 1981 by
THE MACMILLAN PRESS LTD
London and Basingstoke
Associated companies in Delhi Dublin
Hong Kong Johannesburg Lagos Melbourne
New York Singapore and Tokyo

Typeset by Oxprint Ltd, Oxford

Printed in Great Britain by
J. W. Arrowsmith Ltd, Bristol

British Library Cataloguing in Publication Data

Retreat from power.
  Vol.2: After 1939
  1. Great Britain – Foreign relations –
20th century
  I. Dilks, David
  327.41   DA566.7

ISBN 0–333–29319–3
ISBN 0–333–29320–7 Pbk

Contents

The illustration on the jacket shows some of the key figures involved in British foreign policy after 1939: Mr Ernest Bevin; Mr Winston Churchill; Mr Anthony Eden; Mr Harold Macmillan. The first three of these are reproduced by kind permission of the BBC Hulton Picture Library.

Preface

THIS second volume of studies in Britain's foreign relations begins with the Second World War. In some respects, that cataclysm confirmed and deepened the results of the First; Germany and her allies were again defeated. It reversed other consequences, for Russia, having escaped defeat by the narrowest of margins, emerged as the predominant power in central and eastern Europe. No country mobilised its resources of industrial output and manpower more effectively than Britain. Had it been possible to bring the war to an end, say, eighteen months earlier, her political weight inside the coalition would have been much greater than it proved to be in the last year of the struggle. But so enormous an effort, impossible without the support of the United States, inevitably meant that Britain could no longer sustain the whole range of her former burdens, especially when it became clear again that the ending of a great war was not to be followed by a period of peace, rebuilding and good will among the victorious allies.

These essays are intended to show how Britain conducted her relations with foreign powers during the war, with particular emphasis on the United States and the Soviet Union; and how she reacted to the changed circumstances of the uneasy truce after 1945. Professor Gopal's paper provides in some senses a complement to Dr Hillmer's account, given in the first volume, of Britain's adjustment to a new relationship with the countries of the old empire; while Professor Gowing's description of the British government's decision to manufacture the atomic bomb connects naturally with Dr Spiers's review of the factors which the British government had to weigh before deciding in the summer of 1980 to remain a nuclear power, a decision which – quite apart from its significance in the field of armaments – tells us a good deal about the role which the British aspire to play in the international politics of the next ten or fifteen years.

A part of the late Lord Strang's contribution appeared in *International Affairs* long ago. Some years later, he generously provided the whole essay for the use of students here and welcomed the proposal that a survey found so useful by them should be made generally available. I have tried to furnish footnote references for the main points in his text, with information about some of the sources which have recently become available. Then in slightly different forms, Professor Gowing's paper appeared in *The University of Leeds Review*, and mine in the *Transactions of the Royal Historical Society*; the other parts of the book are published for the first time.

Miss Katherine Riley and Miss Irene Cassidy have given invaluable help in the tracing of documents. I should like also to express on behalf of all the contributors warm thanks to our most helpful publishers at Macmillan, and especially to Miss Sarah Mahaffy and Miss Susan Dickinson.

School of History   DAVID DILKS
The University of Leeds   9 August 1980

Introduction

DAVID DILKS

INTERNATIONAL power, by its nature relative rather than absolute, is not easily measured. There are moral and spiritual ingredients which cannot be tabulated; as Churchill observed, when recounting the celebrated remark 'The Pope! how many divisions does he have?', Stalin might have borne in mind a considerable number not immediately visible on parade. Among the tangible elements which make up the strength of the state are its armed forces, the will to use them and their suitability for the most likely tasks; defensibility of frontiers and lines of communication; its alliances; economic and financial sinews; internal cohesion, the sense of unity and identity; efficiency of administration; the quality of political and military leadership; luck.

If Germany was again weaker at sea than her opponents when the war came, she had greater power in the air; but British production had risen rapidly in 1939 and the gap was beginning to close. Germany had the non-aggression pact, but not an alliance, with Soviet Russia. It brought Hitler considerable benefits, for Germany by extracting materials from Russia could render the blockade less effective and thereby nullify to some extent her opponents' advantages at sea. But Hitler's deal with Russia had left his partners of the anti-Comintern Pact in an absurd posture. The Japanese government fell; Italian reluctance to fight increased; and the agreement with Russia did nothing to enhance Germany's influence in those countries where Roman Catholic sentiment was strong. This was of particular importance in Spain, where General Franco made himself as disagreeable as possible to the western allies but persistently refrained from allowing German troops to enter Spain and assault Gibraltar.

'Diplomacy in war', Sir Edward Grey wrote during the earlier struggle, 'is futile without military success to back it. In time of war military success is to diplomacy what heavy artillery, with plenty of munitions, is to an army in the field.'[1] In the first phase, before the allied defeats in Norway, Belgium and France, the balance of advantage was by no means clear. Whatever doubts might be entertained on the British side, the Cabinet and Chiefs of Staff had not realised how readily German armour, with air power in close support, might bundle France out of the war. Even in May 1940 the Chiefs of Staff told the Prime Minister that by bombing and economic strangulation they hoped to produce such crippling shortages in continental Europe that widespread starvation would ensue before the winter and 'by the same date depletion of oil stocks will force Germany to weaken her military control in Europe or to immobilise her armed forces'. In the autumn of that year, after the collapse of France and the Battle of Britain, the Chiefs of Staff were still hoping to produce such privations in Europe that revolt might be stimulated and a British army of thirty divisions able to re-enter the Continent by 1942.[2] Such was the store set by the weapon of blockade, the efficacy of which seemed to have been proved in the First World War. There was a crucial difference, however, a yardstick of Britain's relative decline in a quarter of a century. Not only were she and the Commonwealth countries now left to fight alone, by contrast with the early days of the First World War when Britain, France and Russia waged war together, but there was no longer any hope of paying for this effort. As the British ambassador said to American journalists in 1940, 'Boys, Britain's broke, it's your money we want.'

That Roosevelt was well disposed nobody doubted. However, his good will found only a limited expression until after the presidential election at the end of the year. The fact that the United States showed little sign of intervening, even when France capitulated and Britain was apparently near the last gasp, lends no credence to the view that skilful handling by the British in the 1930s would have brought America into the struggle at an earlier date. The President soon after his reelection determined to offer lend–lease, using the metaphor that if he saw his neighbour's house on fire, it would be no more than common prudence to offer a hose. These measures of economic support proved crucial to the British war effort. Reverse lend–lease, granted by Britain and the Commonwealth countries to the United States from 1942, was in proportion to their resources as generous; in finite terms far less. In those palmy days, British applied science stood in many respects far ahead of American. Beside their expertise in atomic physics, the British supplied in the autumn of 1940 a trunkful of scientific secrets so vital that they were described by Roosevelt himself as the most valuable cargo ever to reach American shores.

That the western powers should pummel each other to exhaustion suited Russian theory and practice ideally. For all his later claims of prevision and intimate knowledge of French rottenness, it is almost certain that Stalin misjudged the prospects. What was happening in 1939–40 fitted Russian needs until the conquest of Scandinavia and the collapse of France altered the European equilibrium decisively. Russia had helped to set for Britain and France the very trap which she always accused them of trying to set for Russia; the deflection of the German military machine while bystanders profited from neutrality. A remark of the Russian ambassador in London of those days, M. Maisky, puts the point perfectly; he always added up the allied and the German losses, he said, in the same column.[3]

From a British point of view, it would have been better that Germany and Russia should fight each other than that Germany should turn on France and Britain. Yet the British had not attempted to encourage anything of the kind. The guarantee given to Poland, lying between Germany and Russia, demonstrates that there was no intention of deliberately diverting Germany eastwards. Moreover, on all that the British were told about Russia's military power, much of which appeared to be corroborated by her performance during the Finnish war, such a course would have been pointless; a German attack on Russia might well have provided Hitler with another triumph, and with increased resources with which to turn against the West. The ambassador in Moscow, Sir Stafford Cripps, a stern unbending opponent of 'appeasement', urged at one stage in 1940 that the British should give way to Russia on most points in contention and (as the diary of the Permanent Under-Secretary expresses it)

> trust to the Russians loving us. This is simply silly. Agree to tell him to sit tight. . . . Extraordinary how we go on kidding ourselves. Russian policy will change exactly when and if they think it will suit them. And if they *do* think that, it won't matter whether we have kicked Maisky in the stomach. Contrariwise, we could give Maisky the Garter and it wouldn't make a penn'orth of difference.[4]

Italy's entry into the war, and the prospect that the French fleet might be captured, meant that for the first time the British had actually to face the risk which had preoccupied ministers before the First World War; namely, the naval strength of all the western European powers arrayed against her. The decision to seize the French ships at Portsmouth and Alexandria and to bombard the battle-cruisers at Oran had both a practical significance in preventing a tilting of the naval balance which the British could not afford, and a psychological import, for it was the act of a government determined to fight with desperation to the last. Six months later, Churchill said that he believed Oran had been the turning-point; it had made the rest of the world realise that the British were in earnest.[5]

It may well be that Britain should have instituted a rigorous blockade, or declared war against Italy in September 1939, so as to deter Italy or to inflict the utmost damage on her fleet and air force while western Europe was comparatively quiet. For understandable reasons, the Chiefs of Staff and War Cabinet had felt that they could not afford to make enemies gratuitously. Nor, for a considerable period after June 1940, could they spare the strength to deal faithfully with Italy. The consequence was a perilous position in the central Mediterranean, unbearable losses to the convoys, the repeated battering of Malta, and grave harm in the Middle East, the only theatre in which the allies could mount a major campaign after ignominious expulsion from France. At least Mussolini's decision gave an occasion for inexpensive relief to the emotions at a time when everything was collapsing. 'We are . . . told that the Italian

Navy is to come to gain sea superiority in these waters', said
Churchill with splendid impudence in Parliament.

If they seriously intend it, I shall only say that we shall be
delighted to offer Signor Mussolini a free and safeguarded
passage through the Straits of Gibraltar in order that he
may play the part which he aspires to do. There is general
curiosity in the British Fleet to find out whether the Italians
are up to the level they were at in the last war or whether they
have fallen off at all.[6]

The British continued their retreat before Japanese
demands. There the essentials of the position remained for
nearly twelve months. The war effort received indispensable
help from America; Britain maintained mastery of the Channel
and the North Sea; and courageously diverted substantial
forces to the Middle East. The much-improved intelligence
services reported the concentration of German forces in eastern
Europe and had accurate information in good time about the
date of Germany's irruption into Russia. Stalin refused to
believe it. In that summer of 1941, Britain took decisions as
critical as those of September 1939 or June 1940: to give military
help to Russia, and in effect to allow policy towards Japan to be
determined by America. It is easy to understand that Great
Britain, fighting for her life, could not afford to take the
initiative against Japan but found it tolerable to share the
risk with the United States. On 26 July 1941, the American
government instituted economic sanctions, and were followed
by the British and Dutch. Roosevelt and his colleagues,
realising by the autumn how effective the economic pressure
was proving, decided against any relaxation. They knew that
Japan might fight rather than submit. Considering the severity
of the policy, the United States' military and naval precautions
were not nearly adequate; and when the Japanese decided to
attack the American fleet at Pearl Harbor, they determined the
outcome of the war. The price paid by the Americans and the
British was a very heavy one indeed; but without the Japanese
action (for Hitler and Mussolini, showing a lack of sense of
proportion as startling as their fidelity to engagements,
declared war on America), it is impossible to see how the

dictators in Europe would have been defeated.

The American Secretary of State remarked to Anthony Eden in 1943, 'I will not say that, if our two nations are in accord, all our problems can be solved; but I will certainly say that without that condition none are soluble.'[7] It was no simple matter for the British to co-ordinate policy with America. The ambassador in Washington, Lord Halifax, much given to sporting images, used to remark mournfully that to do business with the American government was like a disorderly day's rabbit-shooting; if the dog were put down one burrow, the rabbit would appear from another. The President handled a great deal of foreign policy himself, or through intermediaries. Antagonisms between the Secretary of State and some of those with whom Roosevelt preferred to deal were known to the British and had to be accepted, whatever the inconveniences.

The fount and pivot of British power in the Far East, the fortress at Singapore, fell in 1942 not because the heavy guns could fire only seawards, but on account of the disaster at Pearl Harbor and the loss of sea command. That the Americans should nevertheless give priority to the campaign in North Africa and Europe owed a great deal to the persuasiveness of Churchill and the British Chiefs of Staff, and was a decision of the first magnitude. Despite the disagreements between the British and American governments, the essential fact is that they generally reached acceptable compromises. Nevertheless, there is some evidence that Roosevelt felt jealous of Churchill and did not look forward to his visits, because the Prime Minister knew much more about military questions and kept terrible hours. American distaste for the empire, and the alarmingly simple notions entertained on the subject even by leading American statesmen, caused friction and after the war became a source of real weakness to the British. The President seriously advanced proposals for India based upon the experiences of America in the eighteenth century. He urged that the British should give up Hong Kong as a gesture of good will to China, and had in mind a number of such offers; to which Eden retorted that he had not heard the President suggest any similar gestures on America's part.[8] As the Prime Minister remarked, states with no overseas colonies may rise to moods of great elevation and detachment about the affairs of states which have. 'What about those *wretched* Indians?' an earnest American lady asked at dinner in the White House. 'Madam,' he replied when she could no longer be ignored, 'do you refer to the second greatest nation upon earth, which under benign and beneficent British rule has multiplied, flourished and prospered exceedingly, or do you refer to the Indians of the North American continent, who under successive administrations have been reduced to beggary, starvation and extinction?'

*

When Eden went to Moscow just before Christmas 1941, with the Germans almost at the gates of the city, Stalin asked for the frontiers of that year, including a large part of eastern Poland and the Baltic States. Poland would in turn take a good deal of territory from Germany. At the moment when Russia was thought by many to be at the point of defeat, Stalin had advanced the demands which remained the basis of Russian policy to the end of the war. These were essentially the claims over which the alliance was to break up. Eden pointed out to the Cabinet that when Germany was defeated, France would remain for a long time a weak power; there would be no counterweight to Russia in Europe; and Russia's policy would depend upon the position at the end of the war, which no one could then predict. Britain could not gamble on the proposition that Russia would end the war so exhausted that Stalin would have to adopt a policy agreeable to the West. To induce the Americans to become more flexible was at that stage of the war – by almost ironic contrast with the events of 1945 – a serious problem. 'Soviet policy is amoral; United States policy is exaggeratedly moral, at least where non-American interests are concerned.'9

Eventually, the British were able to make a treaty with Russia which omitted mention of the frontiers. This brought a temporary relief from an embarrassing question, but no more. Whether Russia had a grand design to set up communist regimes all over Europe no one knew. President Roosevelt asked the British Foreign Secretary this question in the spring of 1943. Eden replied that he could not tell; but even if the apprehension were correct, the position would not be made any worse by trying to work with Russia.[10] On balance, the British were until 1945 apt to believe that misunderstandings, rather than genuine differences of philosophy or policy, had needlessly divided Britain from Russia in the past. Churchill and his colleagues knew that they were dealing with a pitiless tyrant, guilty of almost unimaginable crimes. Hardened professional politician that he was, Churchill all the same retained a high regard for Stalin. Even at Potsdam he was saying 'I like that man.'[11]

British ministers held no firm conviction of Russian ill-faith. When awkward questions were raised, the necessities of war were held to overwhelm any nice scruples; understandably so, for Russia was engaging an enormous German army. When an official of the Foreign Office suggested that it was terrible for the British, who alleged themselves to be fighting the war for principle and the rights of small states, to be on friendly terms with a power like Russia which had murdered thousands of Polish officers in the Katyn Forest, the Permanent Under-Secretary pointed out that the Soviet Government had long made a habit of butchering its own citizens by the tens of thousands,

> and if we could fling ourselves into their arms in 1941, I don't know that Katyn makes our position more delicate. The blood of Russians cries as loud to Heaven as that of Poles. But it's very nasty. How can Poles *ever* live amicably alongside Russians, and how can *we* discuss with Russians execution of German 'war criminals', when we have condoned this?[12]

Important as the differences of emphasis between Britain and America were, the notion of far-sightedness about Russia on the part of the British, contrasted with naïve optimism on the part of the President, will no more stand up to dispassionate scrutiny than the tale of a distinctively British strategy by which the allied armies would have thrust into south-eastern and central Europe, at the expense of the second front in western Europe. The fact is that Churchill, Eden and the War Cabinet did not come to any consistently apprehensive or hostile view of Russian policy, at least until 1945. With no reason to anticipate that American forces would remain long in Europe in peace-time, the British were chiefly concerned to prevent a German resurgence, an object in which they hoped to find common ground with Russia. A paper put to the Cabinet by the Foreign Secretary expresses the dilemma clearly:

> I assume that the aim of British policy must be, first, that we should continue to exercise the functions and to bear the responsibilities of a world Power; and, secondly, that we should seek not only to free Europe, but to preserve her freedom. Here in Europe, after all, is the cradle, and until recently the home, of the civilisation which has now spread to almost every corner of the globe. Here, too, we have to live, a few miles from the Continent. We cannot afford a Europe unfriendly to our interests or antagonistic to our way of life. We cannot afford a Europe which is dominated by Germany.
>
> For my part, I do not think it is possible seriously to dispute these two objectives. We have to maintain our position as an Empire and a Commonwealth. If we fail to do so we cannot exist as a world Power. And we have to accept our full share of responsibility for the future of Europe. If we fail to do that, we shall have fought this war to no purpose, and the mastery of Europe which we have refused to Germany by force of arms will pass to her by natural succession as soon as the control of our arms is removed. . . .
>
> If it is agreed that these are our objectives, how are they to be realised? It will be admitted, I think, that we cannot realise them through our own unaided efforts. We can only hope to play our part either as a European Power or as a world Power if we ourselves form part of a wider organisation. . . . No international organisation will be effective if the Great Powers are at loggerheads. And whether we are thinking in terms of the United Nations or of the League of Nations it is desirable that there should be the fullest possible understanding and co-operation between the Great Powers. If there is not this co-operation, then I can see a prospect of a world in precarious balance with the Great Powers, each with its circle of client States, facing each other in a rivalry which will merge imperceptibly into hostility.[13]

For all that has been written since, there is not a scrap of evidence that the British and Americans could have invaded France successfully in 1943; even twelve months later, it was a close-run thing. Meanwhile, the Prime Minister had to bear the Russian reproaches with as much patience as he could muster. On one occasion he refused to receive a message from Stalin; he placed it firmly back in the hands of the ambassador and bade him a pointed good-day, describing the document learnedly as 'nul et non avenu'. Churchill recorded in the summer of 1943 that he was becoming rather tired of repeated Russian scoldings, 'considering that they had never been actuated by anything but cold-blooded self-interest and total disdain of our lives and fortunes'.[14]

However, the critical facts remained that to contain Germany Russian help was vital; if Europe was to have a peaceful future, the British and the Russians must get on; and the prospect of open Russian hostility, with a defeated France and a prostrate Germany lying between Britain and the Red Army, could not be called inviting. Moreover, the British were full of admiration for the heroic defence made by Russia, and realised that she had done what Britain could never do, had broken the back of the German Army. But there was the question of Poland. Because the British had gone to war on account of the guarantee to Poland, the issue could not be ignored with a grimace. Thus by stages during 1944 and 1945 Russia's behaviour over the Polish question became the touchstone of good relations between Britain and herself. The allies had already made, in effect, large concessions of territory at Poland's expense, in the well-based belief that Russia would not accept frontiers shallower than those across which she was invaded in 1941. Poland would be compensated at Germany's expense. It was understood that somehow there must be a Polish government friendly to Russia. In the spring of 1944, Eden had minuted on a Foreign Office paper, 'Is Soviet regime one which will ever co-operate with the West?'[15] This was a genuine, not a rhetorical, question.

British influence in the political counsels of the allies ebbed away as the military balance altered. At Moscow in October 1944, Churchill rounded on the Poles and threatened that if they did not behave more reasonably, they would no longer be supported. Stalin said that he and Molotov were the only two in the Russian government who were 'favourable to dealing "softly" with Mikolayczyk. I am sure', Churchill telegraphed, 'there are strong pressures in the background, both party and military.' After this observation, surprising when we remember the general view that Stalin held undisputed sway, the Prime Minister added that he was impressed with Russia's determination to attack Japan once Hitler was overthrown; 'when we are vexed with other matters', Churchill wrote, 'we must remember the supreme value of this in shortening the whole struggle.'

As on other occasions, Churchill was moved by Stalin's apparent friendliness. 'We have talked with an ease, freedom and intimacy never before attained between our two countries. Stalin has made several expressions of personal regard which I feel sure were sincere. But I repeat my conviction that he is by no means alone. "Behind the horseman sits dull care."' [16]

At the Yalta Conference early in 1945, Stalin played his strong cards admirably. The Prime Minister and Foreign Secretary had to weigh their obligations on the Polish question against the urgent need to secure agreement on others. Had the British ministers firmly believed that Russia would behave as she soon did, suppressing 'unfriendly elements' and making nonsense of declarations about the liberation of Europe, the Prime Minister would never have uttered the ringing words about Russia's good faith which Lord Strang records. Within a few weeks, Churchill was sending messages of increasing solemnity and alarm to Roosevelt, by then so feeble that he could not deal with his business. As a sad entry in Eden's diary for 23 March indicates, the British had built a great deal on hopes of collaboration with Russia after the war: 'I take the gloomiest view of Russian behaviour everywhere. . . Altogether our foreign policy seems a sad wreck and we may have to cast about afresh.' [17]

The military position of the British and Americans improved markedly from the end of January 1945, a fact which may have contributed to the desire of the Russians to seize as many positions as possible in central and south-eastern Europe. This they did with a brazen disregard for their partners' opinions. Since it was clear that Germany would collapse in a matter of weeks, the incentive for Russia to buy western good will had largely disappeared. The war-time alliance had been created by no spontaneous sympathy or resolve to stand and fight, of the kind which had brought the Dominions to Britain's side. Nothing short of a German invasion would have brought Russia and Britain to the same side; nothing short of a Japanese assault, we may surmise, would have brought the United States into the war.

Assumptions about the post-war world were dissolving. It became more evident with every passing day that the essential problem might not be the containment of German aggression, but the containment of Russia; how this problem was even to be contemplated, when the United States was likely to withdraw its armies within a year or two, the British did not know. Even before the perfection of the atomic weapon, flying bombs and rockets meant that the Channel could be over-leapt more easily than by aircraft. Attlee wrote in 1944, 'We are not a semi-detached country, free if we will to turn our backs on Europe and look towards the Atlantic, but a continental Power with a vulnerable land frontier.'[18] This was not written with Russia especially in mind, but Russian behaviour in the last twelve months of the war gave point to the policy which Attlee advocated, a close defensive alliance between the countries of western Europe and Scandinavia; conversely, the development of the atomic bomb and airborne weapons went a considerable way to nullify the strategic advantages of the rampart of states with which Russia was surrounding herself in Europe.

As Goering had remarked shortly before the end, the English had entered the war to prevent Germany from going into the East, not to have the East come to the Atlantic. The 'German problem' had remained unresolved after the First World War because of the decision not to enforce a partition of Germany. Much the same issue faced British ministers who reflected upon this question during the Second World War. They were hardly to know that as matters turned out there would be no peace treaty, and that Russia would effectively resolve the question by dividing Germany. They would have been incredulous if told that within a few years Britain and the United States would be promoting the rearmament of Germany.

*

The Western allies have been upbraided for the policy of unconditional surrender without which, it is argued, Germans opposed to Hitler would have had greater reason to overthrow him and the cohesion of the German war effort might have crumbled away. Indeed, beliefs of this kind have become with some authorities almost a matter of faith. The view is not capable of proof or disproof; but 'unconditional surrender', also announced for Italy, did not prevent forces hostile to Mussolini from coalescing, and the formula was not in practice applied to Italy. There was never any likelihood that Hitler and his regime could come to terms with the West. If conditional surrender had been preferred, any terms to which the Americans, Russians and British would agree were bound to be severe in the extreme. It is not clear that an announcement to that effect would have done anything to diminish Germany's astonishingly stubborn resistance.

Before the allies assembled at Potsdam in July, Russia was in military control of the capitals of central and south-eastern Europe, and had already taken large quantities of plunder from east Germany. Polish claims to a line further west than the British had wished were in practice admitted. Churchill, who had been succeeded as Prime Minister by Attlee, records that he had intended to come to grips with the Soviet government over a catalogue of decisions, and would have faced a public break rather than allow the extended western frontier of Poland. But the Russian forces were there, the British and Americans would certainly not fight to dislodge them, and there is no sign that at any stage Russia had valued British good will above physical security and expansion. We may take two sentences spoken during the Potsdam Conference as an epitome of the new conditions. The first was spoken by Stalin and the second by the new British Foreign Secretary, Bevin. 'In my opinion, policy should be based on the calculation of forces.' 'I'm not going to have Britain barged about.'[19]

In these latter years of the war, the British had been finding from revenue not much more than half of their expenditure. They had sold almost all their foreign investments. Their debts were enormous. Starving Europe had somehow to be fed, cities and homes rebuilt. The Potsdam Conference was hardly over before the United States abruptly cut off lend–lease. Of course, the British had known that sooner or later this problem would have to be faced. Churchill had said robustly during the war that he would not mind being asked by the Americans whether Britain could repay:

> I shall say, yes by all means let us have an account if we can get it reasonably accurate, but I shall have my account to put in too, and my account is for holding the baby alone for eighteen months, and it was a very rough brutal baby . . . I don't quite know what I shall have to charge for it.[20]

In August, the Labour government received a paper by J. M. Keynes. It showed how heavily Britain had been enabled to overspend. Even with optimistic calculations, the Treasury could not foresee equilibrium before 1949, and then only by a sharp increase of exports, large cuts in overseas expenditure, strict control of imports, and rationing. And to reach that state further substantial help would be needed from America; without which Britain would be 'virtually bankrupt, and the economic basis for the hopes of the public non-existent'.[21] This was addressed to a government whose principal plank in the election had been the promise of nationalisation and large social reforms. The weakness of Britain's economic position, and acute difficulty over the balance of payments, therefore reappeared immediately as a large factor in the making of foreign policy. Happily for the ministers, they could not foresee the extent and rapidity of Britain's economic and political enfeeblement; or that within a generation or so, defeated and partitioned Germany, quarrelsome and mismanaged France, would be much richer than Great Britain.

There was nothing for it but to turn to the United States anew. Keynes, who had negotiated many of Britain's financial arrangements with the United States during the war, apparently felt confident that he could get £1,500 million as a gift (presumably as an expression of American thanks for holding that troublesome baby) or as an interest-free loan. The shrewd Foreign Secretary said reflectively, 'When I listen to Lord Keynes talking, I seem to hear those coins jingling in my pocket; but I am not so sure that they are really there.'[22] Had the negotiations taken place, say, twelve months later, the task of the British would have been simpler; for they would have been able to take advantage of a much enhanced American fear of Russia. As it was, neither the gift nor the interest-free loan could be got. Arguing with no wheedling mendicancy, lucidly and soberly, Keynes set out to convince the Americans that Britain was a great power which it was in America's interest to sustain. He knew that many of his audience felt little enthusiasm for the prospect of helping to fund the Labour government's domestic programme. Not all his political masters in London understood much about negotiations with American financiers. Keynes had a style in the drafting of telegrams not common in Whitehall. 'We are negotiating in Washington, repeat Washington;' he reminded the Cabinet in early November, 'fig leaves that pass muster with old ladies in Threadneedle Street wither in a harsher climate.'[23]

The terms eventually agreed provided for a loan of $3,750 million at two per cent, to be repaid in fifty annual instalments from the end of 1951. These were terms which Keynes had earlier characterised as the policy of Temptation, of least resistance, which might at first prove agreeable since it would mean that Britain could get out of the immediate difficulty with comparative ease; but bound to bring the day of reckoning, when the upshot for the United Kingdom might well be bankruptcy, 'an outrageous crown and conclusion to all that had happened during the war'.[24] No doubt the circumstances with which he had actually to grapple in Washington were worse than he had imagined. He could not tell that the loan would be gobbled up in little more than twelve months and exhausted by August 1947. It is well to be reminded that Canada, with a population one tenth of that of the United States, made a loan of $1,250 million.

There were many features of the American agreement unpalatable in London. If an entry in the Chancellor of the Exchequer's diary is to be taken literally, he at least had assented to the terms knowing that Britain would not fulfil them:

> My cynical and secret reflection on the American Loan is that we shall be able to make good use of the dollars – though we wish there were more – but that it is quite certain that the

conditions will have to be 'revised' long before A.D. 2001 and
that, even in the next year or two it may well be that circumstances will require a considerable variation, which might
even be 'unilateral'.[25]

And yet for a country dependent upon imports, and therefore
upon the capacity to earn the currency with which to pay for
them, the alternative to American help was hardly conceivable:

> We should go deeper into the dark valley of austerity than
> ever during the war. Less food — except for bread and
> potatoes — in particular less meat and sugar; little cotton and,
> therefore, less clothes and less exports; and worst of all from
> the point of view of public morale, practically no smokes since
> 80% of our tobacco costs dollars. Very soon, after a tre-
> mendous patriotic upsurge, the tide of public feeling would
> turn. Everywhere the Tories would exploit the situation,
> attributing every shortage to the Government's incompe-
> tence. We should be on the downward slope, leading towards
> defeat at the next election.[26]

Had the unfortunate Chancellor been able to count on the
speedy re-conversion of industry, reduction of the armed forces
to modest levels and rebuilding of international trade, he might
have found some grounds for confidence. However, the intransigence of the Russians, the uncertainty of American intentions,
the determination to remain a great power in more than name,
the immensity of Britain's responsibilities, all caused his need
for economies to be counterbalanced by the pleas of the Chiefs
of Staff and Foreign Secretary.

In the first few months, Bevin hoped that it would be possible
to reach some accommodation with the Russians, to slough off
some features of the old diplomacy and conduct matters more
openly, with cards on the table face upwards. He quickly
learned that no technique could be more unsuitable with
Molotov, to whom he tried to teach (without conspicuous success) 'The more we are together'. Tiring of Molotov's obstruc-
tiveness, Bevin said that he would ''ave it out' with him. For
a little while, results seemed to be good; but quite shortly,
Molotov said to Bevin with conscious or unconscious humour

(for part of the government's platform in the General Election had been that it would be better able than the Conservatives to deal with Soviet Russia), 'Churchill and Eden used to be friends with the Soviet Union, but you and Attlee are old-fashioned British Imperialists.'[27]

A meeting of the Foreign Ministers in Moscow just before Christmas 1945 did little more than preserve a façade of polite relations. The British saw more clearly than ever the advantages of bringing France into the equation; but a disinclination to treat France as a first-class power was shared by the Americans and Russians and as Bevin once remarked to the Cabinet, 'the French did not improve the situation by their tendency to make claims disproportionate to their present strength'. British diplomatic contacts with France were already close and cordial, which was more than can be said for much of the war-time relationship; Bevin believed the French apt, instead of building up their international position by piecemeal agreements, to insist on raising major questions not ripe for international settlement.[28]

The new weapons and the uncertain future of the United Nations Organisation pointed to a further dilemma for which no one had a convincing solution. If the international organisation was to be trusted, it must be able to deter aggression more successfully than the League had done. How was this aim to be reconciled with the atomic bomb, even in its first form so vastly more destructive than any weapon previously invented, against which there was no efective defence then known and which could be dropped from an aircraft flying several thousand miles? The argument, carried to its conclusion, meant that the UN itself must be prepared to use such weapons to crush aggression. This was indeed the view of some senior British ministers, who reasoned that it would be idle merely to invent rules designed to secure that war, if it came, should be conducted without the use of the new weapon.[29] But only the Americans had the bomb, and they soon declined to share their knowledge or research. In the autumn of 1945, Molotov, who had drunk a great deal, claimed that Russia also possessed the bomb;[30] but this was discounted. When ministers eventually decided that Britain must have the bomb, Attlee, a thorough master of parliamentary business, showed an impressive knowledge of the administrative machine by smuggling through the estimates the large sums needed for manufacture, disguised under innocuous and misleading headings.

It had been recognised that the UN must command the allegiance of the great powers and could not enforce international peace if they were in fundamental disagreement; hence the system of the security council and the veto. But even by the time when the UN began its work, the chasm separating those powers had become obvious enough. The Russians demanded the evacuation of British forces from Greece; Bevin retorted that the real danger to peace lay in the unceasing propaganda of Moscow and communist parties everywhere against the British people and the government. The Chancellor of the Exchequer fired off to his colleagues 'a flaming warning about the state of Britain's overseas deficits'.[31] Its natural corollary would be further reductions of British troops, bases and commitments abroad; and for some time the Prime Minister had been brooding about the possibilities of a British withdrawal from the Mediterranean. Attlee pointed out that the Commonwealth and empire was not a unit which could be defended by itself, but had been the creation of sea power. 'With the advent of air warfare, the conditions which made it possible to defend a string of possessions scattered over five continents by means of a Fleet based on island fortresses have gone.' He had at first argued that the empire could be defended only by its membership of the UN. If the new organisation were a reality, it would not matter who held the former Italian possessions (Cyrenaica and Somalia) or controlled the Suez Canal; 'if it is not a reality, we had better be thinking of the defence of England, for unless we can protect the home country no strategic positions elsewhere will avail.'[32]

In writing thus, Attlee was reinforcing the experience of both world wars. This paper was composed in the late summer of 1945; and within a few months Attlee himself would have admitted that the assumptions about the UN already looked unreal. However, the Prime Minister in mid-February 1946 was still inclined to think that the British could not keep open the Mediterranean route in time of war. The news was not entirely unwelcome to the Chancellor, who immediately saw that in that event Britain could pull out her troops from Egypt, the rest of the Middle East and Greece, and abandon any thought of defending Turkey, Iraq or Persia against a steady pressure of the Russian land masses. Since the independence of India was clearly not far off, there was therefore still less point in thinking about imperial communications through the Suez Canal:

> We should be prepared to work round the Cape to Australia and New Zealand. If, however, the U.S.A. were to become interested in Middle Eastern oil the whole thing would look different. Meanwhile the U.S.A. seem to be exactly repeating their post-last-war experience. The little men are nominally in charge and the whole political machine is out of control.[33]

The suggestion of withdrawal from the Middle East could hardly have been less timely, for it coincided exactly with severe Russian pressure upon northern Persia. Still the Senate had not approved the American loan; but Keynes felt confident, telling the Chancellor that the only witnesses appearing before the Senate Committee in a contrary sense had been 'three hand-picked lunatics with straw in their hair'. The Pope, it was reported, had also come over to the side of the British and had instructed cardinals in the United States that nothing should be done to weaken British power to resist communism. Even Mr Joseph Kennedy, who had previously been against the loan, had been saying that the British ought to have had it as a free gift and the Irish Americans generally had been told to keep quiet.[34]

The budget of 1946 provided for higher spending on housing, family allowances, pensions, cost of living subsidies, school milk, universities and other areas of social policy; the Chancellor fondly hoped that reductions in defence and connected overseas expenditure would pay for some of this. 'If I could export so many million tons of coal a year,' Bevin used to say wistfully, 'I could put our economy right and have an independent foreign policy.'[35] He has been a good deal mocked for this remark, and unjustly so. His essential point – that without a solid base of economic strength the country would be continually handicapped in its conduct of foreign affairs – was entirely sound. The government recognised that Britain could not hold on to some of her responsibilities much longer; in the case of India, promises of British withdrawal had been made, and only the date was in question; in the instance of Greece and Palestine, withdrawal was more directly related to immediate economic weakness. Whereas over Palestine the British had precious little help and a good deal of hindrance from the United States, in the instance of Greece the British decision to leave was shrewdly timed, when the United States was willing to shoulder new burdens.

Ministers had to ask themselves the same kind of question about Russia as their predecessors had asked ten years earlier about Germany. Was Soviet Russia a power of unlimited ambition? Would she establish puppet regimes by subverting other states from within? Would she use her preponderance on land to launch an outright military attack? Relieved of the danger from Japan, would she be the more adventurous in Europe? Bevin said boldly that he 'would not have the bomb in the Foreign Office' and did not intend to let his policy be deflected one way or the other by the atomic bomb and its possible uses.[36] This he could afford to say, since it was possessed for the moment only by the United States. As for dealings at a high level with the Russian government, they were almost always in the hands of Molotov, whom the Permanent Under-Secretary of the Foreign Office had judged during the negotiations of 1939 'an ignorant and suspicious peasant',[37] an expression which Cadogan did not intend as a description of Molotov's social origins. Another well-placed observer, noting Molotov's invulnerability and imperturbability even under the most vigorous assault from his fellow foreign ministers, was reminded of a hippopotamus he had once seen at London Zoo, massively indifferent to the petty distractions of bystanders.[38] Bevin said that Molotov was just like a communist in a local Labour party; if treated badly, he made the most of the grievance, and if treated well he put up his price and abused his benefactor the next day.[39] Clark Kerr, who had enjoyed exceptional opportunities to judge the Russian leaders at first hand during the war, went as ambassador to Washington afterwards and believed the Russians were not planning world domination, but rather were striving for more security as they conceived it:

They are a very difficult and bad-mannered people; like a
pup which is not house-trained, they bounce about and bark
and knock things over and misbehave themselves generally,
and then next day are puzzled if one is still resentful. They
still have a terrible sense of inferiority. They like, therefore, to
be treated very nicely in public and it does nothing but harm
to shout at them in public; on the other hand shouting in
private often does good.[40]

The Chancellor continued to warn of Britain's economic
weakness. 'As you know,' he wrote to Attlee towards the end of
1946, 'we shall be on the rocks in two years unless we can
redress our balance of payments.'[41] The Prime Minister still
saw attractions in placing a wide stretch of desert and Arabs
between Britain and Russia, and we know that Bevin was much
attracted to the notion of a great strategic reserve in East Africa,
probably at Mombasa.[42] However, negotiations with Egypt
broke down in 1946 chiefly because the Egyptian government
would not allow the prospect of independence for the Sudan.
But for that, the Canal Zone base might have been abandoned
by Attlee and Bevin, rather than by the Conservative government under Eden's impetus in 1954. With each year, the
increasing dependence of Britain upon oil from the Middle East
made a complete military withdrawal more improbable. When
Attlee again made that proposal early in 1947, all three Chiefs
of Staff said that they would resign if it were pressed; and the
idea thereupon lapsed.[43]

Simultaneously, Dalton conveyed his grave concern about
the failure of the Cabinet to grip the essentials of the economic
situation. 'This huge expenditure of manpower and money on
Defence is making nonsense both of our economics and our
public finance.' In another paper of the same period, he had
said that Britain could not afford the money or the men for
which the Minister of Defence asked:

We are vainly trying, in every sector of the national
economy, to do more than we can. Unless we relax, the result
will be rupture. We must think of our national defence, in
these hard and heavy years of transition, not only against the
more distant possibility of armed aggression, but also against

the far more immediate risk of economic and financial over-strain and collapse.[44]

Dalton was saying to his colleagues what Chamberlain had said in 1932, and was trying to do what the governments of the later 1930s have been so sternly rebuked for doing; namely, to judge the maximum sum which could be spent on defence and then to spend it as little ineffectively as possible, trying to attune the commitments to economic reality. At one time and another, almost every administration since those days has had to follow the same course. 'What shall it profit Britain', asked Dr Dalton, 'to have even 1,500,000 men in the Forces and Supply, and to be spending nearly £1,000 millions a year on them, if we come an economic and financial cropper two years hence?' The Ministry of Defence had asked for £963 million; the Chancellor offered £750 million and was told by someone in the Cabinet's discussion that to spend this sum and to have only 1,400,000 engaged in the services and their supply would amount to 'unilateral disarmament'.[45] Eventually, a considerably smaller sum than Dalton would have wished was taken from the estimates.

Fears about Russia, and the financial and other embarrassments of maintaining the British zone in Germany, were transforming intentions which the War Cabinet had formed even a short while before. While the British wished to prevent a German menace to the peace of the world, they also wished to see Germany self-supporting, and the burden upon Britain thereby reduced. Just as the Chancellor was reaching his wits' end, General Marshall, Secretary of State, made a speech which showed that the United States might offer economic aid to Europe on a scale which would greatly hasten recovery. This lifeline was thrown just in time. Russia made all kinds of conditions, most of which were unacceptable. Bevin insisted that the broad issues of principle should be thrashed out, and if necessary made the breaking-point. He confessed to relief when the Russians decided not to come in, for they would have been provided with opportunities to delay and obstruct. 'They may do their best to mobilize European countries against the French and ourselves as things are; but at least the gloves are off, and we know where we stand with them.'

Russia also showed hostility towards other countries wishing to take advantage of Marshall aid. 'If the Soviet government persists in this attitude, European relations will have entered a new phase of tension. . . .'[46]

It would perhaps be truer to say that affairs had already entered this new phase. The British had made a treaty of alliance with France, to last fifty years. A few days after Bevin circulated the memorandum cited above, the Committee of European Economic Co-operation was established; the American and French governments alike, after direct experience of Russian tactics during 1947, moved closer to the position which Bevin already occupied; and early in 1948, the Brussels treaty provided for the defence of western Europe, as well as for closer collaboration in the economic and cultural spheres. All this owed a great deal to Bevin, who had perhaps a more unfettered control of policy than any other Foreign Secretary of recent times. He knew well enough that the countries of western Europe by themselves were in no condition to contain Russia, if that was indeed the task that lay ahead. Again he determined to speak candidly to Molotov. 'What are you after?' he said.

Do you want to get Austria behind your Iron Curtain? You can't do that. Do you want Turkey and the Straits? You can't have them. Do you want Korea? You can't have that. You are putting your neck out too far, and one day you will have it chopped off. We know much more about you than you imagine. We know that you cannot stand a war. But you are behaving in such a way that one day there will be a showdown.

There was apparently a good deal else in the same sense. Bevin argued, reasonably enough, that nobody in his right mind in Britain or the United States wanted a war with Russia; but if war did come between Russia and America in the West, Britain would be on America's side. 'Make no mistake about that. That would be the end of Russia and of your Revolution. So please stop sticking your neck out in this way and tell me what you are after. What do you want?' To this Molotov replied somewhat surprisingly, 'I want a unified Germany.'[47]

The tone of memoranda and remarks by the Foreign Sec-

retary to the Cabinet in 1948 became notably more urgent and
definite where Russian policy was concerned. 'We shall be hard
put to it', he wrote at the beginning of the year,

> to stem the further encroachment of the Soviet tide. It is not
> enough to reinforce the physical barriers which still guard
> our Western civilisation. We must also organise and
> consolidate the ethical and spiritual forces inherent in this
> Western civilisation of which we are the chief protagonists.
> This in my view can only be done by creating some form of
> union in Western Europe, whether of a formal or informal
> character, backed by the Americans and the Dominions . . . I
> am aware that the Soviet Government would react against
> this policy as savagely as they have done against the Marshall
> Plan. It would be described as an offensive alliance directed
> against the Soviet Union. On this point I can only say that in
> the situation in which we have been placed by Russian
> policy, half measures are useless. . . .[48]

The coup in Czechoslovakia and an increase of Russian
pressure on Finland led Bevin within a few weeks to describe
the Russian threat in terms reminiscent of those used before the
war about Nazi Germany. The Foreign Secretary said that the
Soviets had been carrying on a war of nerves; and the recent
events had convinced him that Britain should now go beyond
the original intent of a limited approach to the Benelux
countries, with France, on the basis of the Treaty of Dunkirk:

> It has really become a matter of the defence of western
> civilisation, or everyone will be swamped by this Soviet
> method of infiltration. . . . There is only one conclusion to
> draw. After all the efforts that have been made and the
> appeasement that we followed to try and get a real friendly
> settlement on a four-power basis, not only is the Soviet
> Government not prepared at the present stage to co-operate
> in any real sense with any non-Communist or non-
> Communist-controlled Government, but it is actively
> preparing to extend its hold over the remaining part of
> continental Europe and, subsequently, over the Middle
> East and no doubt the Far East as well. . . . The immensity

of the aim should not betray us into believing in its impracticability. . . .

Bevin accordingly recommended a much closer co-ordination, not only in the military sphere, with France and other allies. He also suggested that a major Russian move would follow within the next few weeks or months. Bevin's proposals were generally agreed by the Cabinet early in March 1948. A point of considerable interest was made in the discussion but not recorded in the circulated minutes: 'We should use U.S. aid to gain time, but our ultimate aim should be to attain a position in which the countries of western Europe could be independent both of the U.S. and of the Soviet Union.'[49] This foreshadows one of the chief arguments advanced for the creation, and later for British membership, of the European Economic Community.

Not long afterwards, the Russian government severed all land traffic of the allies into Berlin, a city surrounded by the Russian zone of Germany; a step taken after it became evident that the western allies were looking to establish a federal republic in West Germany, and to its integration within the economic system of western Europe. Lord Strang, Permanent Under-Secretary of the Foreign Office from February 1949 and Bevin's devoted admirer, said that the Berlin crisis placed upon his master a strain from which he never completely recovered. No one could tell whether it might come to peace or war. Bevin confessed, when tension was at its height, that he now understood what agony Chamberlain must have gone through in September 1938; and that while he would not be one to throw a stone at Chamberlain, he had for himself no thought of yielding over Berlin. Lord Strang adds that Bevin, unlike Chamberlain, had Hiroshima behind him.[50] He had even more than that; what was rapidly becoming a solid commitment from the richest power in the world, translated into an enormous effort for the better part of a year to use air transport in defeating the blockade of Berlin. Bevin told the Cabinet it had been felt that to yield to Soviet pressure there 'would lead to further withdrawals by the Western Allies and in the end to war. On the other hand, if we maintained a firm attitude, we might reckon on ten years of peace during which the defences of Western

Europe might be consolidated.'[51]

No more in 1948 than in 1938 could ministers know whether they would shortly be waging war. Though almost every meeting of the Cabinet was informed of the country's apparently endless economic ills, there is no sign of flinching. The economic and political aspects could not be separated. The point was forcefully made in the Cabinet's discussion on 22 September that if the threat of war in the near future was real, Britain should be devoting more resources to defence, including civil defence; but that tactic would play into the hands of the Soviet Union by retarding Britain's economic recovery. 'On the other hand, it would be fatal to give the Soviet the impression that the United Kingdom would not in any circumstances oppose them by force.' Bevin said he hoped there would be no weakening:

> Since 1945 it had repeatedly been shown that any concessions to the Soviet Union would be exploited to the detriment of the Western Powers and, unless a firm stand was now made, our position in Europe would be hopeless. He also reminded the Cabinet that the economic recovery of West Germany, which had been promoted by the recent currency reform, should to a considerable extent relieve the strain on the United Kingdom's economy.
>
> The Cabinet approved the policy pursued by the Foreign Secretary. . . .[52]

The Berlin blockade was perhaps the most obvious test of strength between 1945 and the Cuban missile crisis in 1962. Neither issue had much to do with theoretical rights. Both had everything to do with will to use or threaten armed force. Britain's contribution to the air-lift was in relation to her resources extremely large, about a third of the flights and a quarter of the supplies. Before the crisis ended, the North Atlantic Treaty had been signed, bringing in not only the United States and Canada, but also Iceland, Italy, Norway and Portugal at the extremities of Europe; in addition, of course, to France and the Benelux countries. This was perhaps the most weighty act of British foreign policy since the war. To tie the United States to the defence of Europe was visibly an advance of the first importance; had it been possible to foretell how rapidly the gap in wealth, productive capacity and technical expertise would widen between Britain and the United States, the act would have seemed more important still. NATO has provided the main focus of British defence policy, especially since the abandonment of empire in the late 1950s and earlier 1960s, and the most enduring theme of Anglo-American political collaboration.

It is not to be imagined that this close relationship with the United States extended to foreign policy all over the world. Palestine, and the Middle East generally, provided the most glaring example of disunity between the two powers. The question of Palestine, in which the British role was unheroic for sheer lack of the resources to command the situation, and in which the government found itself faced with the intransigence of Arabs and Jews alike, did great harm to Anglo-American relations. The government's military and political advisers, said one minister at the Cabinet, had been seriously over-estimating the strength of the Arab states; Britain would have done better to base her position in the Middle East upon the friendship of the Jews who, if a different policy had been pursued, would have been glad to give facilities for military bases in Palestine. Other ministers countered that there was no reason to believe that Israel would be specially favourable to Britain; and in any case the connections of the Commonwealth with the Muslim world made it essential that Britain should support fair treatment for the Palestine Arabs.[53]

In the late summer of 1949 Bevin defined the British interest in the Middle East in terms which would have been unhesitatingly endorsed by the Conservative Foreign Secretaries of the 1950s:

> In peace and war the Middle East is an area of cardinal importance to the United Kingdom, second only to the United Kingdom itself. Strategically the Middle East is a focal point of communications, a source of oil, a shield to Africa and the Indian Ocean, and an irreplaceable offensive base. Economically it is, owing to oil and cotton, essential to U.K. recovery.
>
> In addition to these vital strategic and economic interests, His Majesty's Government have weighty responsibilities

towards the peoples of the Middle East, by history, tradition
and in some cases by treaty. Our influence is greater than
that of any other foreign power. It is essential that we should
maintain our special position and carry out our special
responsibilities.

. . . In a major war the active partnership of the U.S. would
be of supreme importance. In peace, economic development
and refugee resettlement are impossible without large-scale
U.S. participation. Alignment of policy with the U.S. is
accordingly essential. This need not necessarily involve the
loss of our special position. . . .

Our aim must be that the whole of the Middle East,
including both the Arab countries and Israel, should have
close and friendly relations with the West, but if we were to
gain the friendship of Israel at the expense of losing our
position and influence in the Arab countries, we should lose
more than we should gain. We must therefore hold the two if
we can.[54]

This paper the Cabinet approved as a general directive to the
Foreign Office. It did not explain what was to happen if the
alignment of policy with the United States could not be
reached; or what was to be done if close and friendly relations
with the Arab states on one side and Israel on the other proved
incompatible. These were in fact the conditions of the 1950s.

The other area of the world in which notable divergences of
policy arose between Britain and the United States was the Far
East. As the forces of Chiang Kai-shek were expelled from the
mainland, one of the props of American post-war policy collapsed. The British had no desire to drive a Chinese communist
government into the arms of Russia. Hong Kong could not be
held against attack by a major power operating from the
mainland. The British authorities in the Far East wished to
form a containing ring against further communist expansion by
the action of India, Burma, Siam, French Indochina and the
Dutch East Indies. The Foreign Secretary himself had often
expressed a desire for closer political co-operation: but the
proposal for common action between those powers raised every
sort of difficulty. The colonial policies of France and Holland
in the Far East were not regarded with favour by the British

government. Moreover, though it is not clear that the Cabinet realised the point at first, the idea of a containing ring (if it meant co-ordination of foreign and military policy) in which India would be a leader ran contrary to the stance which the government of India had adopted in international affairs. Nehru had advised privately that in Asia communism would be most dangerous where it could ally itself with nationalism.[55]

The political and military authorities in the Far East again urged that failure to meet a threat to Hong Kong would shake British prestige throughout the East. A common front against communism in Siam, Burma and Malaya would probably crumble unless the peoples there were convinced of British determination and ability to resist the threat. In earlier discussions, the Cabinet had felt reluctant to commit themselves to a long-term defence of Hong Kong. Attlee, Bevin and other ministers considered how a decision to defend Hong Kong could be presented in such a way as to command the support of public opinion in democratic countries. Attlee told his colleagues that he had concluded it should be presented as a decision to resist aggression and he recommended that support for such a policy should be enlisted from the governments of other Commonwealth countries and the United States. The arguments which reverberated in the Cabinet had many echoes of the later 1930s. It was rightly pointed out that if a strong communist government were established in the whole of China, Britain could not maintain Hong Kong as a trading centre unless that government acquiesced, as in practice it has done ever since. If it were made a point of prestige to retain Hong Kong as a British possession, it might equally become a point of prestige for the communists to force British withdrawal. On the other hand, it was argued that if the British showed no determination to defend the colony, the risk of attack would increase. If the British did show themselves resolved to stay there, the communist government was unlikely to maintain an economic blockade for any length of time, because the continued interruption was likely to be as embarrassing for China as for Hong Kong. Moreover, there would be other consequences if Britain showed vigour; the anti-communist front in south-east Asia would be strengthened. The Cabinet by this stage had more realistic information about the likely attitude of

India. A declaration by Nehru of support for the policy of defending Hong Kong would be inconsistent with his opposition to colonialism, and with the policy of neutrality. The Cabinet agreed in the end that the future of Hong Kong should be discussed with the government of China only when it was friendly, stable and in control of a united country. By the end of the year, the British government had decided to accord early recognition to the communist government of China, but had to acknowledge that British and American policy could not be harmonised.[56]

Although collaboration between Britain and her Commonwealth partners had been close during the war, its course had perforce strengthened their consciousness of dependence upon the United States. Australia and New Zealand had felt the Japanese threat in what the British called the Far East and they called the Near North. The Commonwealth countries had deliberately taken a large share in the Far Eastern campaign. Nevertheless, they could not conceivably have defeated Japan without the alliance of the United States; and although all the panoply of imperial power reappeared in Burma, Malaya and Singapore, the foundations of British dominion had been undermined. Moreover, the promise that India should be free of British rule implied an opportunity to leave the Commonwealth. Burma took that step. India and Pakistan, after delicate negotiations to reconcile their determination to have republican constitutions with the position of the Crown, became members. This was a decision of the highest significance. It made possible the transformation of the Commonwealth; the example of India and Pakistan certainly strengthened the argument for early independence of other countries; and the plans for zones of Commonwealth defence stretching from the western borders of India to Australasia had to be abandoned. India had for a long time provided what the rest of the empire notably lacked, a strategic reserve of troops able to move west or east.

Curiously, the effect of Indian independence upon the rest of the colonial empire was hardly appreciated at first.

The British perhaps did not readily realise how deeply their standing had been sapped by the disasters of the Far Eastern war, or how the international pressures (including those of the

United States) to abandon empire would increase. When Mr
Creech-Jones, Colonial Secretary in the Labour government,
consulted Governors of British territories, the general view was
that Britain still had as much as forty or fifty years before her as
a colonial power, at any rate in Africa;[57] and this when the
independence of Ghana lay only a decade away.

*

Under Bevin, with the steadfast support of the Prime
Minister, Britain played an international role greater than the
country's material strength warranted. Before the Labour
government left office, the Korean war had darkened the prospects yet further; the country embarked upon a programme of
rearmament so extensive and bearing so heavily on the
economy that by an irony Churchill, the incoming Prime
Minister, had to reduce it. There was a sense in which the
comparative cheapness of the atomic weapons, and British
possession of the capacity to make them, appeared to redress
the imbalance of force with Russia. Moreover, two great wars
had been fought in a lifetime with the United States neutral
for prolonged periods. The emphasis on the nuclear arsenal
implied a theory of deterrence akin to that which the British had
developed in the days before the war, when it had been thought
that there would be no effective defence against bombers; the
ability to inflict heavy damage must be so clearly established
that aggression would not be risked.

This period during which the British regularly exercised a
disproportionate influence in foreign affairs perhaps extended
for some twenty years after the Second World War. In his last
phase as Foreign Secretary, Sir Anthony Eden showed constructive imagination and diplomatic skill in a series of difficult
issues: the crisis caused by the Persian seizure of the Anglo-
Iranian oil company's installations at Abadan; a patiently-won
settlement after the collapse of French resistance in Indochina;
the restraining of the American Secretary of State, Mr Dulles,
who showed some wish to intervene there; an agreement with
Egypt which effectively protected the rights of the Sudan and
provided for British withdrawal from the Canal Zone; the
acceptance of German rearmament, a commitment of at least

four British divisions to Europe for a period of fifty years, and the creation of Western European Union.

It is natural to look for simple explanations when a great power has lost its position swiftly, or to discern some flood which, taken at the tide, would have reversed fortune. It has been widely stated, for example, that the British could have made their own conditions if they had realised early enough the significance of the movement towards economic integration in Europe. This is most improbable. States, particularly when their own vital economic interests are in play, do not commonly act in gratitude for the past. Britain could certainly not have written the terms without the good will of France, and it is very hard to see how Britain's ideal terms could be easily reconciled with French interests then, or for that matter now. The projects for European economic integration in 1956 were in fact carefully studied and weighed. Mr Macmillan, then Foreign Secretary, had long been an advocate of closer links between Britain and Europe; but as he pointed out to Parliament, Britain felt the pull of three distinct forces: the Commonwealth tie, on which no small part of Britain's economic and financial strength depended; the geographical and cultural link with Europe; the alliance with the United States. He argued that the British must try to find a way of supporting greater unity in Europe, but without running counter to their other interests. France, Germany, Italy and the Benelux countries had by that stage agreed to work towards a customs union which would abolish tariffs against all goods within it and impose a single common tariff against all the goods of the outside world. If the United Kingdom joined, he argued, her own tariff would be swept aside and the goods coming in from the Commonwealth would pay duty at the same rate as goods from any third country:

Judged only by the most limited United Kingdom interests, such an arrangement would be wholly disadvantageous. We could not expect the countries of the Commonwealth to continue to give preferential treatment to our exports to them if we had to charge them full duty on their exports to us. Apart from that, our interest and responsibilities are much wider. I do not believe that this House would ever agree to our entering arrangements which, as a matter of principle, would prevent our treating the great range of imports from the Commonwealth at least as favourably as those from the European countries . . . I feel sure that the Governments of the countries who are negotiating their Customs union in Brussels understand and appreciate our position in this matter. So that is out.[58]

Developing countries in the Commonwealth would clearly not remove their tariffs against European goods, and European countries, lacking British links with the Commonwealth, would not grant free entry to Commonwealth manufactures. The Cabinet therefore looked to arrangements by which a group of other countries would be able to associate with the customs union, but with large safeguards for Commonwealth interests. The details of the proposals do not concern us here and were eventually overtaken in the later negotiations; but the view which the speech expresses was very widely held by people of all persuasions. So rapidly has the Commonwealth faded from the forefront of political business in Britain and from the general consciousness that it is very hard for a later generation to appreciate what it still meant then.

The fact that Mr Macmillan's government also was able to wield a large influence, especially after President Kennedy succeeded Eisenhower in 1961, indicates that it was not Suez which marked the end of Britain's time as a great power or, as imaginative commentators sometimes suggest, constituted Britain's Vietnam. The process of decline was a longer and subtler one than that. It is unlikely that military intervention by Britain and France in the Middle East in 1956 would have been contemplated had the British been able to secure a close working relationship with the United States over Middle Eastern policy. That prize eluded each Foreign Secretary in turn, Bevin, Morrison, Eden, Macmillan and Selwyn Lloyd. Mr Khruschev, having greeted with open contempt the announcement of France that she would not seek to become a nuclear power,[59] made himself perfectly affable to the British in most respects, showed no appetite for adventures beyond the iron curtain in Europe, but said in so many words during his visit to Britain in 1956 that Russia would stir up as much trouble as possible for the British in the Middle East. He understood very well, of course, how dependent the British had become upon the supply of oil and its transit through the Suez Canal. He was told by Eden, then Prime Minister, that the oil was vital to Britain and that she would fight for it.[60] What Suez did demonstrate was that the British government of that time was not prepared to abandon the use of force in pursuit of its national interests; a miscalculation of the attitude of the United States, expected to be one of somewhat indignant neutrality but not of active hostility; and the vulnerability of Britain to the economic pressure exercised by the United States. That Suez imposed severe strains within NATO and the Commonwealth is indisputable. On the other hand, the worst of the damage to both associations, and more particularly to the relationship with the United States, was repaired. Mr Macmillan's government sought in a European free trade area an alternative to the developing economic community, and to play British cards above their value in relations with Russia and America, whom the British tried earnestly to reconcile. Perhaps the realisation that Britain could not exert enough leverage to press the two greatest powers effectively, and induce them to follow more sensible courses (as they appeared to British eyes), had more to do than any other factor with the decision to seek entry into the EEC. Certainly the transformed Commonwealth by then offered no alternative base of power.

More than a decade separated the original application from the acceptance of British membership. In one sense, entry into the EEC confirmed what both world wars had shown, that however hard she might try, Britain could not avoid an intimate involvement with the affairs of Europe. Whether British membership will engender a full-hearted commitment to the development of the EEC as a supra-national institution is debatable, for long-established instincts and attitudes are not quickly altered. The EEC is not NATO, and it is upon NATO that British defence still rests. Relations with France, paradoxically, remain less cordial than they were twenty-five years ago. Britain's relative economic decline has been so marked as to undermine both her capacity and her will to play a major part in international politics. It would in any event have to be played in much-changed circumstances, for the margin of

American superiority in nuclear weapons, a shield for western Europe, has disappeared; Russia has become a great sea power as well as the dominant land power; China has re-entered the international community and appears to cause in Russia a profound apprehension somewhat akin to that which was once created by Japan; the dependence of the industrial nations upon imported oil has been alarmingly demonstrated; President Carter has declared the Persian Gulf a vital interest of the United States, to be defended by force if need be, much as the British Foreign Secretary did in 1903; and by her own direct intervention, as in Afghanistan, or through surrogates, as in south-east Asia and the horn of Africa, Russia has shown herself adept in exploiting the gaps left by the retreat of other imperial powers.

Britain remains a small and densely populated island, not able to feed more than half its people, dependent upon overseas supply but, thanks to the discovery of oil, with at least the hope of a more healthy economy if the imminent period of extreme danger in international affairs can be surmounted. Even if she wished, Britain could not wisely concentrate her economic, political and defensive effort solely upon western Europe; yet it would be hard to deny a marked narrowing of British horizons in the last fifteen or twenty years. A former American Secretary of State, Mr Dean Acheson, remarked that Britain had lost her empire and had not yet found a role. The aphorism was much resented. At a distance of twenty years, we may have the grace and humility to admit that it held a good deal of substance.

1. The Twilight War and the Fall of France: Chamberlain and Churchill in 1940

DAVID DILKS

ONE evening early in the war, the First Lord of the Admiralty and Mrs Churchill invited the Prime Minister and Mrs Chamberlain to dine. By a happy chance the conversation turned to Chamberlain's early life in the Bahamas. He told the story of the struggle to recruit the family's fortunes by growing sisal on a remote and windswept island in the Bahamas, 'living nearly naked, struggling with labour difficulties and every other kind of obstacle, and with the town of Nassau as the only gleam of civilization'. Chamberlain described how, for all his exertions, the scheme had failed. In the Chamberlain family, it was felt that though they loved him dearly they were sorry to have lost £50,000. 'I was fascinated', Churchill recorded after the war, 'by the way Mr. Chamberlain warmed as he talked, and by the tale itself, which was one of gallant endeavour. I thought to myself, "What a pity Hitler did not know when he met this sober English politician with his umbrella at Berchtesgaden, Godesberg, and Munich that he was actually talking to a hardbitten pioneer from the outer marches of the British Empire!"'

That this should have been the first conversation of its kind in an acquaintance of nearly forty years, and that Churchill should hitherto have known nothing but the barest outline of Chamberlain's early life, tells us a good deal about the distinctions of habit and temperament between the two. They had been close colleagues, but never on terms of intimacy, in Baldwin's second government from 1924 to 1929, and despite occasional frictions and a mutual recognition of differences of approach and style had worked fruitfully together then. During the decade which separated Churchill's departure from the Exchequer from his return to the Admiralty, disputes over policy between him and his former colleagues had cut deep: his adherence to free trade, his violent dissent over India, altercations about disarmament and the pace of German rearmament, the row over the abdication, outright and unqualified condemnation of the Munich settlement. Yet the evidence is clear that even amidst these clashes Churchill acknowledged the qualities of Chamberlain, whom he justly described in 1936 as 'the pack-horse in our great affairs' and whose unopposed election as leader of the Conservative Party he seconded in the following year. After the guarantee to Poland was given at the end of March 1939, when their disagreements about foreign policy had been much reduced, Churchill intimated plainly that he would like to take office. Acknowledging that the government would profit from the increase in debating strength which Churchill's accession would bring, Chamberlain decided that so long as there was any chance of preserving peace, the gain would be outweighed by the loss. As he recorded in July 1939:

> There are more ways of killing the cat than strangling it and if I refuse to take Winston into the Cabinet to please those who say it would frighten Hitler, it does not follow that the idea of frightening Hitler, or rather of convincing him that it would not pay him to use force, need be abandoned.[1]

A week or two later, after a sharp exchange in Parliament had been quickly smoothed down, Chamberlain recorded again, 'That is Winston all over. His are summer storms, violent but of short duration and often followed by sunshine. But they make him uncommonly difficult to work with.'[2] All the same, there was at least no ideological gulf. 'For the old aphorism "Force is no remedy" I would substitute "The fear of force is the only remedy".' That was written by Chamberlain but might as well

have been written by Churchill. Most of their arguments, in
short, were about practical issues and soon proved susceptible
to the powerful solvent of shared information and shared
responsibility. Both were in a real sense self-taught, and neither
had attended a university. Churchill might have said that he
received his real education in the vacations from Harrow and
the long afternoons of India, and Chamberlain his in the
unavailing struggle to grow sisal and the effort to redeem that
failure by service in the business and municipal life of
Birmingham. Neither was a life-long adherent of the Conservative Party; Chamberlain, after all, was the son of the most
celebrated Radical statesman of his day, and even in Joseph
Chamberlain's later life the divergence between Liberal
Unionism and Conservatism had been marked. Churchill had
once abandoned the Conservative Party for the Liberals, and
had come back, through a succession of somewhat odd trans-
mogrifications, to the Conservative fold in 1924. As he used to
remark with a mischievous twinkle, 'Any fool can rat, but I
flatter myself that it takes a certain ingenuity to re-rat.' Even
after then, however, there remained many strands of his former
Liberalism, especially his devotion to free trade and hostility to
the tariffs, with which Chamberlain was so closely identified by
filial piety and personal conviction alike. Each admired in the
other industriousness, swiftness in the transaction of business,
moral and physical courage.

Here lay the foundations of a collaboration which, despite
occasional disagreements over policy and obvious differences of
character, developed in a fashion which reflects high credit
upon both and which may without extravagance be called
crucial to the war effort of Great Britain in a year when she
survived by a narrow margin the most determined assault made
in modern times upon her interests. Even now, the story is little
known. The belief that Chamberlain and Churchill were always
divided by irreconcilable differences persists strongly, not least
because of the stern strictures passed by Churchill himself upon
his predecessor in *The Gathering Storm*. All this makes it more
necessary, and the more absorbing, to look afresh at the abun-
dant evidence preserved in the official records and Chamberlain's private papers.

In the autumn of 1938, shortly after the Munich crisis,

documents exchanged at the highest level of the government, and approved by Chamberlain, indicated that on the outbreak of a major war the best course would be to form a War Cabinet of about half a dozen members, most of whom would be free from normal departmental burdens. No final decisions could then be arrived at, for none knew when and in what form the crisis might come. The War Cabinet of 1939 was, as Chamberlain expressed it in a private letter, constructed on no theory about its size or nature. 'My sole purpose was to find a Cabinet that would work, which means that *personalities* must be taken into account.'[3] The Prime Minister's first intention had been to give Churchill a seat in the War Cabinet, but without a department. When it became clear that Liberal and Labour oppositions would not serve, Chamberlain reconsidered. In agreement with Churchill, he decided that the three service ministers should have seats in the War Cabinet. On 3 September, he offered Churchill the Admiralty. As the latter remarked in his account of these events, he naturally preferred a definite task to that exalted brooding over the work of others which may well be the lot of a minister who has no department. When Churchill himself became Prime Minister, he had for a time to make genuflections in the direction of the principle that members of the War Cabinet should not be unduly hampered with departmental responsibilities, a theory particularly fashionable in 1939 and 1940. But as he candidly confessed in his memoirs, he did not like having unharnessed ministers around him, preferred to deal with chiefs of organisations rather than with counsellors, and believed that everybody should do a good day's work and be accountable for something definite; 'and then they do not make trouble for trouble's sake or to cut a figure'.[4] Chamberlain, with his excellent administrative grasp and faith in clear lines of responsibility, certainly felt likewise. Moreover, he doubtless reasoned that Churchill would be a less tiresome colleague if given absorbing duties.

It was only at sea that the allies enjoyed a clear superiority. Whatever might be said and written about 'the phoney war', the struggle at sea was waged with unremitting vigour from the start. In many important respects the strategic situation differed from that which had been envisaged even as late as the spring of 1939. The conjunction of three enemies in widely scattered theatres, which the Chiefs of Staff had so long apprehended and which Chamberlain's government had striven to avoid, had not come about. The Japanese showed no inclination to join Germany, and even Mussolini had been convinced in the last days of August that Italy was in no position to fight. On the other hand, Russia had joined hands with Germany, was soon to partition Poland with her, and began to supply raw materials vital to the war effort of Nazism. This latter fact no doubt eased relations between Chamberlain and Churchill, for the latter, having spent a good deal of the spring and summer urging the government to meet the Russian terms, felt deeply affronted by Stalin's decision to join Germany and was soon denouncing communism and its works with all the vehemence of 1919. The British and French governments agreed in the early phase of the war upon three crucial issues: first, to undertake no offensive in the west although a token advance would be essayed in order to offer some comfort to Poland; secondly, to pursue the struggle at sea with all strength immediately, about which there was no choice anyway because of submarine warfare; thirdly, to keep Italy neutral if possible, in order to spare France war on another front, and to preserve the free passage through the Mediterranean upon which the British relied heavily. With these decisions Churchill was in full agreement. All were based on the arguments that time was working for the western allies and that Germany might collapse under internal stresses, or at least find her effort weakened.

For the first six or eight months of the war, the refusal of the opposition parties to join the government proved less of a handicap than might have been expected. The comparative quiet on the western front, and the reluctance of either side to begin aerial warfare, meant that for the moment the government could get by. It had an ample parliamentary majority; it was strengthened by the inclusion of Churchill and Eden, as well as by a number of ministers of high ability from outside, including Lord Woolton and Sir John Reith; and Chamberlain maintained his position without undue difficulty. His parliamentary performances were generally good, his mastery over the business was acknowledged and he managed the Cabinet well. There is no sign that Chamberlain stood in any special awe of Churchill. Although it is common to refer to him as a

Prime Minister who almost always won his point in Cabinet, and not uncommon to see references to Chamberlain's dictatorial control, the minutes and the accounts left by colleagues do not convey that impression. Unlike his successor, Chamberlain seldom spoke first about any important item at the Cabinet, though he would often have discussed the issues with colleagues, in small groups or singly, before a decision was reached. He expected ministers to know their business, and on more than one occasion asked a minister, politely but firmly, to leave the meeting of a Cabinet committee, find the facts desired, and come back with them.

The original arrangements of the War Cabinet were built around three committees, for home policy, civil defence and priorities, each spawning several sub-committees. Soon it was necessary to add a ministerial committeee on economic policy and another on food. As for the military control, the system practised during the First World War had to be accommodated to the establishment of the Chiefs of Staff sub-committee which now reported directly to the War Cabinet. In October 1939 a committee on military co-ordination was set up under Lord Chatfield (Minister for the Co-ordination of Defence). The three service ministers, and the Minister of Supply, were members of this body. The structure meant that each issue of importance had to be tackled three times; by the Chiefs of Staff, then by the Military Co-ordination Committee, then by the War Cabinet. As we shall see, Churchill chafed a good deal under this system; Chamberlain and others, mistrusting some of the First Lord's enthusiasms and believing him too ready to overrule advice, probably thought that the advantages of such checks outweighed the inconveniences. However, this is to anticipate. For the moment, Chamberlain and Churchill alike assumed that the war might be a long one, engaging the resources not only of the British Isles but of the British communities across the seas, and the task was therefore to develop British power over a period of years. There was nothing in the policy of the United States government, though Roosevelt expressed himself affably in private correspondence with Chamberlain and Churchill, to encourage the assumption that the industrial strength of America would be available to the Allies, even if they could not pay. On a sober calculation of the

respective resources, there seemed solid ground for hope. As
Chamberlain put it after a few weeks of war, 'The allies are
bound to win in the end and the only question is how long it will
take them to achieve their purpose.'[5] In assessing such remarks,
which may seem foolish to a degree in view of the events of May
and June 1940, we have to remember that the French army was
judged capable at least of holding the line in the west, if not of a
successful onslaught upon Germany. This opinion was held
even more strongly by Churchill than by Chamberlain.

The new First Lord, who had acknowledged in his speech to
Parliament on 3 September that repeated British efforts for
peace had been not only of the highest moral value but also of
practical value, for the war could not be waged without the
wholehearted support of scores of millions, began at once to
favour Chamberlain with a series, which soon became a torrent,
of letters upon numerous subjects. On all the broad issues they
were at this stage agreed; for instance, Churchill no more
wished than Chamberlain to bomb the Ruhr, to attack Italy, or
to take any step which might provoke the Japanese. 'It seems to
me most unlikely', he wrote to Chamberlain in mid-September,
'that the Germans will attempt an offensive in the west at this
late season.'[6] This was a view which, with some fluctuations,
Chamberlain shared; though we know now that Hitler would
have liked to make an attack in the west, even at a considerably
later date, and was restrained only with difficulty and by the
weather. In all his ordinary dealings, Chamberlain was a most
punctilious correspondent. Because he was seeing Churchill
every day in the War Cabinet, and often at other meetings or in
private, he did not answer each of these missives. At the end of
the letter already quoted, Churchill added:

> I hope you will consider carefully what I write to you. I do so
> only in my desire to aid you in your responsibilities and
> discharge my own.

Chamberlain answered that he did indeed consider all
Churchill's letters carefully, but had not replied in view of their
constant encounters and close agreement. Part of Chamberlain's reply, dealing with an issue central to the war and upon
which it had been impossible to form more than an intelligent

guess beforehand, indicates the care with which he balanced the reports from the theatres of war, the competing needs of the services and the limited economic resources of the country:

To my mind the lesson of the Polish campaign is the power of the Air Force, when it has obtained complete mastery in the air, to paralyse the operations of land forces. The effects in this direction seem to me to have gone much beyond anything that we were led to expect by our Military Advisers, and as a result it seems to me to be above all things vital that we should not allow ourselves to get into the same position vis-à-vis Germany as the unfortunate Poles. There is the more danger of such a catastrophe because the French Air Force is so weak that it does not seem to me to be beyond the bounds of possibility that if the Germans concentrated upon them they might, in a comparatively short time, wipe out not only the French Air Force, but also their means of production of aircraft. This would be a very formidable blow, and although our own Force is now a very powerful weapon, I do not feel confident that it has yet achieved such strength as to ensure that we do not lose command of the air.

Chamberlain's first impression was therefore that the needs of the Royal Air Force should have absolute priority and he did not see how the plans for an army of fifty-five divisions could be reconciled with the needs of the RAF.[7] Churchill pointed out, with justice, that he was anxious for the army to plan on the scale of fifty or fifty-five divisions because he doubted whether the French would acquiesce in a division of effort which gave the British the sea and the air and left France to pay almost the whole of the blood tax on land. 'Such an arrangement', he added brightly, 'would certainly be agreeable to us; but I do not like the idea of our having to continue the war single handed.' To this letter Churchill added in manuscript (and the remark is an index of the close relationship which he and Chamberlain were establishing), 'I am grateful to you for the fuller expression of yr. views, and it is my first desire to be of service to you.'[8] There is no reason to doubt the sincerity of this remark. On the issue immediately at stake, Chamberlain decided to support the conclusion that an army of fifty-five divisions should be raised, despite the immense problems of finance, of manpower, of procurement of machine tools and allocation of resources between the services, entailed by such a decision. When the Cabinet concluded its discussion of the issue, he received from the First Lord the following note:

> My dear Neville,
> I hope you will not think it inappropriate from one serving under you, if I say that in twenty years of cabinets I have never heard a more commanding summing-up upon a great question.

Reporting this compliment, Chamberlain commented, 'I need hardly say perhaps that I had come down in favour of the solution he had advocated.'[9]

No one doubted that Churchill would compile ample memoirs which, though they might rejoice in a grand title, would consist largely of letters and memoranda written by the First Lord himself. It seemed to Chamberlain that some of the papers which he received from Churchill in the first month of the war were so plainly written for the purpose of future quotation, and to prove foresight, that some action must be taken. Indeed, Chamberlain's own letter about the effects of air power in the Polish campaign, already quoted, was written because 'I thought I must get something on the record too which would have to be quoted in the Book'.[10] These communications, which ministers would toss to each other with the exclamation 'another one for posterity', and Churchill's tendency to garrulity and irrelevance in the Cabinet, proved to be the main obstacles to easy collaboration between him and the Prime Minister in the first few weeks of war. On the other hand, they continued to agree on matters of strategy and tactics, while the Prime Minister rightly judged Churchill to be sensitive to personal appeal. Some of the newspapers carried a vigorous campaign in favour of Churchill at the end of the month, widely believed to have been stimulated by Churchill's close friends still out of office and not disapproved by the First Lord himself. Chamberlain in recounting events to his sisters remarked that though he was not seriously alarmed by the effusions in the press, he was becoming very tired with the barrage of letters from Churchill, arriving daily and increasingly devoted to matters outside his sphere of business at the Admiralty.

On Sunday 1 October, Churchill wrote a 'private and personal' communication to the Prime Minister dealing with the size of the army in France; the formation of new RAF squadrons; and ARP defences and lighting restrictions. Given the line which Churchill's friends appeared to be taking in the press, and the fact that this looked uncommonly like another document written for eventual printing in the memoirs, Chamberlain resolved to send for Churchill and put an end to the process. They had what the Prime Minister describes as 'a very frank talk':

> As I expected, he responded at once, withdrew his letter and promised to write no more and swore vehemently that he had no desire or intention of intrigue. That he was quite satisfied with the responsibility he had and wanted no more and that his sole desire was to help me to win the war. I believe all this was quite genuine, though Winston is in some respects such a child that he neither knows his own motives nor sees where his actions are carrying him. But the result was excellent. He went away in the highest good humour and has been extra friendly ever since! Although some of the papers are carrying out a sort of campaign against the composition of the War Cabinet, I don't believe there is anything in it in the public mind and . . . we are working together very harmoniously and successfully.[11]

It is well known that from an early stage of the war Churchill pressed for offensive action in Scandinavia. The emphasis of his arguments, and the purpose of the operations which he proposed, varied somewhat as new facts came to light. The history of these events has been recounted again and again and need not be repeated in detail. What concerns us here is the opinion to which Churchill came about the machinery of Britain's war-time government. It was natural that an ardent, experienced, knowledgeable minister, given to heady enthusiasms and apt to override all but the most strongly-expressed dissent, should search for ways of exploiting the naval superiority of the

allies. There can be no doubt that he exaggerated the effects
which a cutting of the supply of iron ore from Sweden, even if
that could be achieved, would produce on the war economy of
Germany. At various stages, the First Lord proposed the laying
of mines in the territorial waters of Norway, which would mean
an open violation of Norway's neutrality, so that the ships
carrying iron ore would have to use the open sea. At another
moment, he seriously proposed that a barrage of mines should
be laid across the whole of the North Sea. The reservations of
the Foreign Secretary, Lord Halifax, derived partly from a
healthy scepticism about the economic effects of severing the
traffic in iron ore from Narvik, and perhaps rather more from
the conviction that Britain must do everything possible to
cultivate the good will of the neutrals, and especially of the
United States. The whole question entered a new phase when
Russia attacked Finland at the end of November. Chamberlain
and Churchill had been entirely at one in believing that the key
to Stalin's actions would lie in Russia's national interest, or at
any rate in her perception of it. Neither could believe that it
would suit Russia to see Germany supreme in Europe, over-
running the Balkans perhaps and planting herself on the shores
of the Black Sea. The sad history of British and French policy
towards Scandinavia in this period of war twilight, a phrase
coined by Chamberlain and found by Churchill so just and
expressive that he adopted it for the second book of *The
Gathering Storm*, is complicated and it does not lend itself easily
to summary. The Foreign Secretary and the Chiefs of Staff,
anxious as they might be in principle to take advantage of
Russia's attack on Finland – which seemed for a time to offer the
prospects of aiding an aggrieved small power, impressing
neutral opinion favourably, and placing in Scandinavia an
army which would cut off the iron ore traffic – had a still keener
desire not to add Russia to the list of Britain's enemies.
Chamberlain felt likewise, and in his handling of meetings of the
Supreme War Council consistently turned down French suggestions which would have led infallibly to war with Russia.
Even now it is not possible to explain the apparent lighthearted-
ness with which some of these proposals were advanced. Churchill seems to have felt a growing confidence. In his broadcast of

mid-November, before the Russian attack on Finland, he said simply:

> I thought it would be a good thing for me to tell you now how well the war has turned for the Allies during the first ten weeks. It is quite plain that the power of the British Empire and the French Republic to restore and revive the life of the Polish, Czech and Slovak peoples, as well as to do a few other things which I will mention later, has been growing every day . . .
>
> You know I have not always agreed with Mr. Chamberlain; though we have always been personal friends. But he is a man of very tough fibre, and I can tell you that he is going to fight as obstinately for victory as he did for peace.[12]

The First Lord of the Admiralty did not appreciate how damaging would be the effects upon sea strength of unopposed air power. This lesson was to be taught in a terrible way a few months later in Scandinavia; but during that autumn, probably basing himself upon judgements reached during the first war, Churchill insisted upon the planning in outline of an operation called 'Catherine', which would have locked up in the Baltic a large portion of Britain's sea strength, without air support, and on all the showing of later events with disastrous results. Much time and effort were expended before he could be dissuaded. This is not to say, of course, that even if Churchill had been able to persuade his professional advisers, the War Cabinet would necessarily have sanctioned such an operation, for Churchill was not then in a position to impose his will. The example is merely cited to indicate his thirst for offensive action, which he valued for its effect on morale as well as for its practical results, and the dangers of dependence upon a profound study of warfare of a different kind. On the balance, and with every allowance for changes of opinion, Churchill appears to have believed that Britain could by boldness command the northern waters and that if the war were extended into Scandinavia that fact would therefore redound to the advantage of Britain and France and to the disadvantage of Germany, since the latter was profiting with impunity from the neutrality of Norway and Sweden.

So the argument swayed backwards and forwards at meetings of the War Cabinet, the Chiefs of Staff and the Supreme
War Council. More than once it seemed that agreement had
been reached and then some new factor always arose – or so it
seemed to Churchill – to impose a further period of paralysis.
Most of the Cabinet, including the Prime Minister, had by
mid-January 1940 decided against an immediate operation to
stop the ore traffic from Narvik. Churchill, understandably but
not necessarily with right on his side, remonstrated with the
Foreign Secretary about the obstacles to action; the numerous
departments of the government which had to be convinced, the
Joint Planning Committee, the Chiefs of Staff Committee, the
juridical and moral objections, the attitude of the neutrals, the
criticisms in the Cabinet, the French, the Dominions.

> All this makes me feel under the present arrangements we
> shall be reduced to waiting upon the terrible attacks of the
> enemy against which it is impossible to prepare in every
> quarter simultaneously without fatal dissipation of strength.
> . . . One thing is absolutely certain, namely that victory will
> never be found by taking the line of least resistance.[13]

He broadcast robustly about the progress of the war at sea,
declaring that no naval war had ever proceeded so well and that
it seemed 'pretty certain' that half the U-boats with which
Germany had begun the war had been sunk. This was a wild
exaggeration, and one which Churchill uttered against the
advice of the Director of Naval Intelligence at the Admiralty. In
the same broadcast he praised the Finns for exposing, for all the
world to see, the military incapacity of Russia and for dispelling
many illusions. 'Everyone can see how Communism rots the
soul of a nation; how it makes it abject and hungry in peace,
and proves it base and abominable in war.' We may remark in
parenthesis that in view of all this, Churchill required some
hardihood to say loftily in his own account that many people in
Britain congratulated themselves

> that we had not gone out of our way to bring the Soviets in on
> our side, and preened themselves on their foresight. The
> conclusion was drawn too hastily that the Russian Army had
> been ruined by the purge, and that the inherent rottenness

and degradation of their system of government and society was now proved.[14]

This broadcast did much harm among the neutrals. Churchill had insisted upon making it without allowing the Prime Minister or the Foreign Secretary to vet the text and the Ministry of Information said that its work in neutral countries had been set back by three months. Even Churchill indicated to the Foreign Secretary some faint signs of contrition. Chamberlain reflected in private that a heavy price had to be paid for the First Lord's presence in the Cabinet. Of course, all the endless restrictions, inconveniences, harassments of petty bureaucracy and everything else inseparable from rationing and control provided the press and the Opposition with many an occasion to make difficulties. The opportunity was not diminished by the fact that for so much of the time there was comparatively little news of the war. Chamberlain, who was by then almost certainly in the grip of his fatal illness but did not know it, reflected that he sometimes felt there would be compensations in handing over to someone else. 'Only I don't see that other to whom I could hand over with any confidence that he would do better than I.'[15] It may be added that according to all the extant evidence, Churchill would not at that stage have been the candidate preferred by his immediate colleagues in the government, or the Chiefs of Staff and civil servants, or most Members of Parliament.

The one difference of substance between the two men remained the Scandinavian question. Even there, the distinction was a limited one. For instance, Chamberlain and Churchill were agreed that British warships should violate Norwegian territorial waters in mid-February to take the German vessel *Altmark* and release the British prisoners which it was carrying. In the second half of February, while Finnish resistance slowly crumbled away, the issue had to be decided. After uncharacteristic hesitation, Chamberlain came down against the immediate laying of mines in Norwegian waters or the seizure of Narvik. He reached this conclusion not upon any ground of principle but because he wished to do nothing which would prejudice the small remaining chance of permission from Norway and Sweden to go to the aid of Finland. He had also in mind the many Americans who would regard the mining of those waters as an attack on neutral rights, and had not forgotten that a presidential election would be fought in America later that year. Having seen one or two senior colleagues privately before the meeting of the War Cabinet, and told Churchill in advance, Chamberlain broke his usual practice and explained his reasoning at the outset of the discussion. Churchill, disappointed and still convinced that the operation would have been justified, said that the Prime Minister with his special responsibilities must be the final judge. There could be no question of embarking upon such an operation against the opinion of the Prime Minister 'on whose shoulders fell the principal burden of the conduct of the war. In all essentials there was no difference of opinion in the War Cabinet; all of them were equally anxious to strike a blow at Germany. It was better, however, not to act when one was in grave doubt as to the consequence of one's act.' Chamberlain thanked Churchill warmly for this generous attitude, and meant it. The other members of the War Cabinet were of the same opinion as the Prime Minister who, recounting it all with some amusement, recorded that 'the relief of the rest of the brethren was comic. Simon whispered to me, "Splendid! You are a *real* Prime Minister."'[16]

It is not necessary to dilate here upon all the events of the following month. The collapse of Finland dealt a severe blow to the prestige of the allies. Chamberlain, conscious of the damage, sensibly expressed in a private letter his relief that it had not been necessary to send an expedition to Sweden, an enterprise 'of much risk and uncertainty with as many possibilities of disaster for us as for them, and one which would have drained valuable resources which we can use elsewhere. I shall be surprised if Russia, having got all she wanted in the Baltic, does not now rather withdraw from than seek closer German embraces.'[17]

Churchill expressed privately to the Foreign Secretary his deep concern about the progress of the war. Again he protested that any positive project to seize the initiative became enmeshed and strangled by the machinery. Soon the ice would melt, and the Germans be masters of the north:

Can we suppose they have not been thinking about what to do? Surely they have a plan. We have none. There is no sort of action in view except to wait on events. These I fear are taking an increasingly adverse turn. . . . Faithful discharge of duty is no excuse for Ministers; we have to contrive and compel victory.[18]

It is hard to resist the conclusion that a desire to show that Britain and France could seize the initiative, and do more than merely react to the latest German stroke, had much to do with the eventual decision that action should be taken in Scandinavia. The French government urged that the fall of Finland made it the more necessary to control the territorial waters of Norway. This was the common policy of Daladier and of Reynaud, who succeeded him in late March. Well it might be, since the theatre of war would be a long way removed from France and the brunt of the operation would certainly fall on the British. Churchill had meanwhile been pressing an operation which came to be known as 'Royal Marine', according to which mines would be placed in the river Rhine; floating with the current, they would disrupt and ruin transport on the river. The French felt less enthusiasm, fearing immediate German reprisals. However, it was agreed that the action against Norway and the mining of the Rhine should proceed simultaneously. Chamberlain continued to argue that Germany must remain the target, and deflected the French, and to some degree Churchill, from planning the passage of submarines into the Black Sea. However, even Churchill, who was close to Reynaud, found himself embarrassingly caught up in the feud between the latter and Daladier. The French went back upon the decision to execute 'Royal Marine'; and the British decided to proceed regardless with the mining of Norwegian territorial waters. Neither Chamberlain nor Churchill seems to have expected any serious counterstroke by Germany, or to have known that a German attack on Denmark and Norway was imminent.

Meanwhile, in another of his broadcasts Churchill had repeated the conviction that because no great event had occurred in the first six months of the war, the allies had thereby gained an important success, for immense progress had been made in almost every direction in the strengthening of the forces, the improvement of defence, the adaptation of the economy to the service of the common cause. He said in so many words that time had been on the side of the allies, though time was a changeable ally. A day or two later, the Prime Minister observed that after several months of the war he felt ten times as confident of victory as at the beginning and that during the seven months the relative position of the allies towards the enemy had become a great deal stronger. This was the speech in which, using a phrase of which he was rather fond in private, he remarked that Hitler had 'missed the bus', by which he meant that it would have been to Germany's advantage to attack Britain and France at the outset of the war. In short, there was little difference of substance between the Prime Minister's view and the First Lord's, though the latter was not prevented in his retrospective account from describing Chamberlain's utterance as 'ill-judged', and as 'not reasonable' the assumption that Britain and France were relatively stronger than in September 1939.[19] Whatever impression may have been conveyed in later years, the fact is that at this stage Chamberlain and Churchill were closely in line about the policy to be pursued, and of the two Churchill was perhaps the more confident of the Scandinavian operation. He described the German onslaught upon Denmark and Norway as a strategic blunder and felt sure the Royal Navy could deal with it.

It need hardly be said that Chamberlain was conscious of Churchill's dissatisfaction with the machinery of government. He realised that Churchill would like to be Minister of Defence, with authority over the War Office and Air Ministry, and noted on 10 March, 'that just won't do'. This was not a question of personal pique. Chamberlain was told, and there is every reason to believe that he was well-informed, of Churchill's repeated expressions of loyalty and admiration. One of the Prime Minister's letters describes him as being 'in spite of his violence and impulsiveness, . . . very responsive to a sympathetic handling'.[20] When the Minister for Co-ordination of Defence, whose somewhat anomalous position has already been noticed, resigned in early April, Chamberlain arranged that Churchill as the senior service minister would preside over the Military Co-ordination Committee. He was not given authority over the other service departments, but told Chamberlain that he deeply appreciated the confidence placed in him and would try to respond to it. Unhappily, this experiment worked ill. Churchill's own account ascribes that fact largely to failures of the machinery. Chamberlain, by contrast, attributed many of the faults to Churchill's dominating personality, refusal to delegate, and wearing methods of business:

> He goes to bed after lunch for a couple of hours or so and holds conferences up to 1 in the morning at which he goes into every detail, so I am informed, that could quite well be settled by subordinates. Officers and officials in his own and other departments are sent for and kept up until they are dropping with fatigue and Service Ministers are worn out in arguing with him. I say to myself that this is the price we have to pay for the asset that we have in his personality and popularity, but I do wish we could have the latter without the former.[21]

The situation within the Military Co-ordination Committee quickly became so bad that Churchill had to ask Chamberlain to preside. The general conviction, or so the Prime Minister recorded, was that Churchill had ruined a machine carefully built up to ensure that all projects should be thought out and examined by a planning staff drawn from all three services.

> I am bound to say that I don't think Winston did mean to supersede this body, but he does enjoy planning a campaign of an operation himself so much, and he believes so earnestly in all his own ideas (for the moment) that he puts intenser pressure on his staff than he realizes. The result is apt to be that they are bullied into a sulky silence – a most dangerous position in war.

Churchill himself said to Chamberlain, 'They'll take from you what they won't take from me.' The Prime Minister insisted on holding meetings at 10 o'clock each morning and noted that the proceedings instead of lasting for some hours became a good deal more swift and efficient.[22]

Unusually, Chamberlain was more confident of success in

Norway than were the Chiefs of Staff. For a time Churchill shared the mood. He changed his mind with bewildering frequency and was said by the Secretary for War, Oliver Stanley, to have forced the Military Staffs into agreement, on at least one occasion, with a course of which they disapproved. It soon became plain that all the high hopes of the Norwegian campaign would be falsified. In one of his private letters towards the end of the April, Chamberlain recorded that at a meeting late one night of the Military Co-ordination Committee, Churchill had behaved like a spoilt and sulky child, and was not much better at the Cabinet the next day. The Prime Minister knew that Churchill was complaining of being thwarted and of having insufficient powers. They had a talk that evening which produced some effect. Churchill said that he wanted to become Minister of Defence, had no desire but to help and was completely loyal to the Prime Minister. The latter, apprehending some of the difficulties, said that he must see the service ministers and think the position over. No decision in the Norwegian campaign had been taken against Churchill's advice and a number had been taken upon it. Chamberlain observed in the same account that although the First Lord put forward many nonsensical proposals, he very rarely maintained them against reasoned argument. The new arrangements under which each of the Chiefs of Staff had a Deputy, which Chamberlain had just introduced and which he had been particularly anxious to secure, made it a good deal easier for the Chiefs of Staff to discuss matters with the First Lord without stopping the whole machinery of the staff,

> and I am trying to find a way of satisfying him without dangerously weakening the authority of the Cabinet. But this incident has given me many hours of worry and anxiety and I have felt a strong inclination to take my head out of the collar and let someone else do the donkey work. Only I know in my heart that I can't do that but must go on and try my best to fulfil my responsibilities.[23]

Chamberlain saw the Secretaries of State for War and Air and found them both disinclined to accept his proposals, which would give Churchill the power without the responsibility and would therefore fasten on them, or so they feared, the blame for decisions which were his. This, Chamberlain pointed out, was what was happening already, and he was trying to regularise the position and build into it certain safeguards. The two ministers concerned, Sir Samuel Hoare and Oliver Stanley, said that they would rather that Churchill should become Defence Minister, while they would resign and be succeeded by Under Secretaries so that everyone should know where the responsibilities lay. Only when Chamberlain said that he would himself resign and let Churchill be Prime Minister as well as Defence Minister did they reply that this would be too great a disaster and they would do what he asked. Chamberlain then drafted a document which defined the new functions of the First Lord, a paper immediately accepted by Churchill who made no attempt to secure larger powers. He also thanked Chamberlain very warmly for the efforts which he had made to meet his point.

Chamberlain's account of these proceedings indicates strongly that he doubted whether the arrangements would last though he felt sure that Churchill did not wish a breach. Chamberlain also recognised that an open quarrel between them would be a disaster for the allied cause.[24] Under the new dispensation, Major-General Ismay, who had often expressed his alarm about Churchill's irruptions into the field of strategy but who admired the First Lord and worked well with him, was placed in charge of a central staff, made a member of the Chiefs of Staff Committee and generally put at Churchill's disposal. The latter would continue to take the chair at all meetings of the Military Co-ordination Committee when the Prime Minister did not preside, be responsible on that Committee's behalf for giving guidance and direction to the Chiefs of Staff and be empowered to summon the Committee whenever he thought it necessary. The Chiefs of Staff would retain their duty to give a collective view to the government and their individual responsibility to their respective ministers. It is hardly possible to tell how this arrangement might have worked over a prolonged period, for within a week Churchill had become Prime Minister, and the long-awaited German thrust had cut into Belgium and Holland.

Chamberlain has been much criticised for his conduct in the debate of 7 and 8 May, and especially for the use of the word 'friends'. As the immediate context of the remark indicates plainly, Chamberlain was not in the least appealing to his personal or political friends to keep the government in office, though that is the complexion which Lloyd George put upon the words. No doubt the language was unluckily chosen, but at least it was better that the challenge should be openly faced and that there should be no atmosphere of double dealing and intrigue like that which had surrounded Lloyd George's own ousting of Asquith. When it was announced that the majority had fallen to eighty-one, Chamberlain asked Churchill to go to his room. He said he could not go on as Prime Minister and that there should be a national government since one party alone could not carry the burden. Unless someone could form an administration in which all parties would serve, Britain could not get through. Churchill, his combative nature and generous instincts aroused by the noisy circumstances of the debate, in which he had done battle lustily and had trounced the Opposition with the more vigour because he recollected that they had voted solemnly against conscription only four months before the outbreak of war, urged Chamberlain to fight on. 'This has been a damaging debate', he remembered himself as saying, 'but you have a good majority. Do not take the matter grievously to heart. We have a better case about Norway than it has been possible to convey to the House. Strengthen your government from every quarter, and let us go on until our majority deserts us.'[25]

Chamberlain was not comforted or convinced. He knew that he could not form a national government, but was determined that one must be created. It was necessary to secure from the Opposition an official confirmation of this attitude, if only to justify his resignation to the Conservative Party. He put his point to Churchill and Halifax who both agreed. The Labour leaders were thereupon asked whether they would join a government under Chamberlain or, if not, under someone else. The Prime Minister had not mentioned any other name but had understood that the Labour Party would favour Halifax and certainly Chamberlain himself would have done so. However, Halifax had no stomach for the office; Chamberlain was told that the Labour leaders were veering round in favour of Churchill; and the First Lord himself made no secret of his view that the best solution would be for him to take the office of Prime Minister. Two ironies stand out in this chain of events: first, the German onslaught in the west plainly demonstrated that the withdrawal from Norway had been the right course, and that whatever had transpired earlier in the Scandinavian campaign, withdrawal would have been necessary once French resistance failed; secondly, Churchill had a greater responsibility than any other minister for the failures of the campaign, though that is not to say for a moment that different handling by him would have produced an allied victory in Norway. Chamberlain remained Leader of the Conservative Party and one to whom the large majority of his followers were devoted. Churchill had at that stage a comparatively limited following. Clearly he was dependent in the parliamentary sense upon Chamberlain's good will, a fact which he acknowledged immediately upon receiving the King's commission to form a government. His first act on returning to Admiralty House was to write a letter of gratitude to Chamberlain for his 'self-forgetting dignity and public spirit . . . To a very large extent I am in your hands – and I feel no fear of that.'[26]

Chamberlain realised that it would not be possible to follow Churchill's first suggestion that he should take the Exchequer, or the second that he should lead the House of Commons. As he observed, the only chance of allowing the Opposition's hostility to die down was to take a place which did not bring him into conflict with them. He feared, in which apprehension he was by no means alone, that the new Prime Minister's circle of intimates and methods of doing business would be disagreeable. Before the war came, it had been Chamberlain's habit to say that he felt he would have to hand over, if such a disaster happened, to someone else; for he knew what agony of mind it would cause him to give directions bringing death and misery to so many. But the war had proved so different from his expectation that he had found the strain bearable:

and perhaps it was providential that the revolution which overturned me coincided with the entry of the real thing. I confess that I am thankful that the primary responsibility is off my shoulders . . . I must say that Winston has shown up well so far. After one or two hectic nights when we were kept up till the small hours he has reverted to morning sittings of the Cabinet. He does take the opinions of the Staff and doesn't attempt to force different views upon them or to shoulder off his colleagues. Our own relations are admirable and I have no difficulty with any of my colleagues in the Cabinet.[27]

These are the circumstances, creditable to both men, in which the last phase of collaboration between them began. To adapt a remark once made about Campbell-Bannerman, there never was such a change in a man's form as after Churchill's assumption of the office. He rightly detected that the role of Prime Minister suited his temperament and abilities far better than any subordinate post; whereas Chamberlain, recognising that in this more active phase of the war Churchill with his special study and knowledge of military subjects was more qualified to lead the government, went efficiently about his business, without rancour or self pity. The new Prime Minister grew in stature and in character. As Baldwin said, in language as appropriate to an ironmaster as to a lover of monosyllables, the furnace of war smelted out all the base metal from him. Suddenly it had become clear that Britain and Germany were locked in a death grapple and increasingly likely that within a few weeks Mussolini would join in. This was the kind of crisis to which Churchill's talents were suited. He was at his best when concentrating with unremitting energy upon an immediate danger. He had the wisdom, after a certain amount of persuasion, not to tamper much with the machinery which he had inherited in the shape of the Chiefs of Staff, the Vice-Chiefs and the Military Secretariat of the War Cabinet. His position became immensely powerful partly because he was what General Smuts used to call him, the indispensable man because the only one full of ideas, partly because he knew a great deal about warfare and as Minister of Defence had thrashed out most of the important questions of strategy with the Chiefs of Staff before they reached the level of the War Cabinet and, most of all, because he was able to forge in the next few weeks an alliance with the British people, including millions who would never have dreamed of voting Conservative. As he used to remark, his speeches in 1940 were hardly the outcome of deliberate reflection. That was the time when the white-hot glow, overpowering, sublime, ran through the island. The Prime Minister did not do himself justice to say that it was the people who had the lion's heart and he who had the luck to be called upon to give the roar. Churchill was utterly unlike other politicians; something of a buccaneer, something of a show-man, an artist through and through, eager for fame. He knew how to appeal to the emotions, and was not ashamed to display his own in public. The sense of being an island again, of being beleaguered behind the moat defensive, greatly enhanced the sense of unity of a whole nation behind the Prime Minister; in the endearing phrase of the day, 'we are in the final and it is being played on our home ground'.

We know that in the first few weeks Churchill had many doubts whether his government would last. He seems to have relied confidently upon the help of Chamberlain, who from the start presided when Churchill was away. The first such occasion occurred on Thursday 16 May, by which time the news from France was already very bad. When General Dill explained the plans for a withdrawal from Belgium, Churchill sprang up from the Cabinet table and refused to agree to a step which would jeopardise the BEF. He said he must go at once to France. He would leave that afternoon. It was ridiculous to think that France could be conquered by 120 tanks. 'Neville,' he said, 'please mind the shop!' That evening Chamberlain presided over a committee which debated what to do in the Mediterranean if Italy should come into the war. On the next day, he was asked to examine instantly the consequences of a withdrawal of the French government from Paris or the fall of that city, and the problems which would arise if it were necessary for the BEF to leave France.

As for domestic business, Churchill minuted that he wished the handling of economic problems to be placed under the Lord President of the Council. Trade, transport, shipping, the Ministry of Economic Warfare, food and agriculture would all come into one group of activities, over which Chamberlain would exercise 'a large measure of executive control'.[28] On 21 May, Chamberlain presided over a Cabinet committee and proposed that in this emergency the property and service of everyone should be placed at the disposal of the state. The leader of the Labour Party proved distinctly hesitant! However, Mr Arthur Greenwood favoured this measure, as did Halifax. The War Cabinet assented and the whole business passed through Parliament in one day, 22 May, amidst many tributes to the energy and drive of the new administration. It was already clear that the fall of France was a matter of time only. Even Churchill told some of his colleagues towards the end of the month that 'if we could get out of this jam by giving up Malta and Gibraltar and some African colonies, he would jump at it'.[29]

On 28 May, probably because he desired to strengthen his parliamentary position, Churchill sounded Chamberlain about the prospect of bringing Lloyd George into the government. Chamberlain explained with frankness his mistrust of Lloyd George, whose word he did not believe and whose motives he suspected. If the Prime Minister thought that Lloyd George would be the more useful, he had only to say so. It was for Churchill to choose. To this the Prime Minister replied at once that Chamberlain was of far more help. There was no comparison between the two of them, and he himself did not trust Lloyd George and did not know whether he might not be a defeatist.[30] Then began a confused interlude in which Churchill and Lloyd George exchanged letters, the Prime Minister pointing out that he had no party of his own. 'I have received a very great deal of help from Chamberlain. His kindness and courtesy to me in our new relations have touched me. I have joined hands with him and must act with perfect loyalty.'[31] There the matter rested for a day or two. On the last night of May, Halifax and Chamberlain were the only members of the War Cabinet in London and took it upon themselves to instruct General Alexander to withdraw from France as quickly as possible, preferably by the following night, although the French had said that they wished him to hold on for a third night and thus help to get out more of their own troops. This decision was strongly supported by the Prime Minister on the next day.

The disaster to the BEF, perhaps naturally in the circumstances, was seized upon as an occasion to condemn Chamberlain and other survivors of the governments of the late 1930s. This campaign gathered strength in the early days of

June. Chamberlain accordingly told the Prime Minister on the evening of 5 June that if his membership of the government was hampering the national effort, Churchill had only to say so and he would resign at once. Churchill replied that there could be no question of Chamberlain's going. He had only just formed his government and Chamberlain was giving him splendid help. A secret session was expected to be held on the following Tuesday and Chamberlain pointed out that if personal attacks were made on him then, he could not defend himself without attacking Labour members now in the government, particularly Attlee and Greenwood, with whom he was working in complete harmony. This would be an impossible position. Only the Prime Minister could reply and his line would be simple enough; that in Great Britain's deadly peril, it was no time to rake up the past or seek scapegoats. The Prime Minister said that he would certainly speak in this sense; he had given most generous representation in the government to the Labour Party and it would be intolerable if Labour members still carried on attacks against members of the previous government. At Chamberlain's request, Churchill undertook to see Attlee and Greenwood and tell them to call off the attacks in the *Daily Herald*, as they could certainly do. Indeed, he said he would see the press generally and ask them to put a stop to the outcry. He then asked Chamberlain again about the proposal to bring Lloyd George into the War Cabinet, which would 'take away the only possible spearhead of attack on the government'. He thought that personal feelings ought not to be taken into consideration now. 'He would stand by what he had said to me and if his choice was between me and Ll.G. he would choose me; but I ought to ask myself whether it was right that I should put such a choice upon him.'[32]

By the next morning, when the newspapers' attacks had gained in strength, Chamberlain had decided that he must withdraw his opposition to Lloyd George's membership of the government, on condition that the Prime Minister should extract from Lloyd George a direct assurance that on entering the Cabinet he would drop his feud against Chamberlain. Moreover, the outcry must be stopped before any announcement was made about Lloyd George's entry. Lloyd George immediately gave this assurance, but asked for time to think the offer over. From the next day, the campaign in the press was switched off magically.

During the last days of the collapse in France, Churchill told the House of Commons that to hold an inquest on the conduct of governments and parliaments in the pre-war years would be a foolish and pernicious process. As he put it, pithily, 'there are too many in it'. He refused to accept the drawing of any distinction between members of the government, who were going to stand together, govern the country and fight the war.

> It is absolutely necessary at a time like this that every Minister who tries each day to do his duty shall be respected; and their subordinates must know that their chiefs are not threatened men, men who are here today and gone tomorrow, but that their directions must be punctually and faithfully obeyed. Without this concentrated power we cannot face what lies before us.[33]

Chamberlain had learned that morning of a movement, with which the Secretary for India, L. S. Amery, was associated, for the establishment of a committee of safety of three members, to replace the War Cabinet. Several junior ministers were reported to support the proposal. Chamberlain told the Prime Minister, who became very angry and said, 'I shall dismiss them. I shall tell them that if there is any more of this nonsense they will go. We must have discipline in the Government.' He also remarked that he had heard nothing from Lloyd George. Chamberlain said: 'Perhaps he may be waiting to be the Marshal Pétain of Britain,' to which Churchill retorted 'Yes, he might, but there won't be any opportunity. Anyhow he has had a fair opportunity and hasn't taken it, and I shall leave him alone.' That evening, Churchill told Amery that if members of the government wished to criticise its workings or composition, they should resign and criticise from outside. He was going to make no changes and would sooner resign himself than be forced to do so. The Prime Minister also offered to arrange for the resignation of Amery to be accepted in time for him to speak in the secret session a couple of days later.[34] This put paid to the matter. Although it appears that Lloyd George was once again offered a place in the Cabinet he could not make up his mind to accept. He failed to speak in the secret session, at which the Prime Minister defended Chamberlain vigorously. Small wonder that the latter recorded on the next day, 'Winston has behaved with the most unimpeachable loyalty. Our relations are excellent and I know he finds my help of great value to him. But if we suffer further disasters we may all go down.'[35]

Chamberlain exerted himself to emphasise in public and in private the solidity of the government. Since rumours of dissension, or even of the desire of some ministers to parley with Hitler, continued to circulate, Chamberlain broadcast a stern denial at the end of June, saying that those who listened to such idle tales were merely playing the Nazi game:

> We are a solid and united nation which would rather go down to ruin than admit the domination of the Nazis. . . . If the enemy does try to invade this country we will fight him in the air and on the sea; we will fight him on the beaches with every weapon we have. He may manage here and there to make a breakthrough: if he does we will fight him on every road, in every village, and in every house, until he or we are utterly destroyed. . . . We shall be fighting for our own hearths and homes, and we shall be fighting with the conviction that our cause is the cause of humanity and peace against cruelty and persecution, of right against wrong; a cause that surely has the blessing of Almighty God. It would be a faint heart indeed that could doubt of our success.

Churchill wrote to him at once: 'I am vy. much obliged to you for yr. most inspiring and resolute broadcast, wh. I read with the greatest pleasure. I am sure it will do no end of good.'[36]

The defeat in France had a significance far beyond the loss of a vital battle. From a British point of view, it meant a dangerous alteration in the balance of naval power, mitigated somewhat by the decision to seize or sink ships of the French fleet in early July. It taught many painful lessons about the effects which might be produced by well-directed air power. It made Italian entry into the war certain and the British position in the Middle East and the Mediterranean much more precarious. Above all, it signified the defeat of assumptions with which all British governments of recent times had been identified: namely, that France was strong enough to hold Germany on land, and that the greatest British contributions would be made at sea and in the air. No one had believed this more fervently than Churchill, and even he had been a belated convert, though not quite as belated as Chamberlain, to the notion that Britain must raise and equip an army on the continental scale. It is fair to add that in facing this task, ruinous as it proved, Churchill's government had from the end of 1940 a degree of American support hitherto unthinkable.

As Lord President of the Council, Chamberlain continued to deal with a mass of business on the Prime Minister's behalf. Towards the end of July, he was discovered to be dangerously ill. An exploratory operation would be necessary at once, perhaps to be followed by something more serious. This might entail absence for three months, and Chamberlain accordingly offered his resignation. The Prime Minister, very distressed, replied with vehemence that whether it took three weeks or three months made no difference; Chamberlain must stay in the government. The first operation revealed a serious cancer. Churchill treated his colleague with exquisite consideration and sympathy. Even in the Battle of Britain he found time to despatch papers and messages to the house in Hampshire where Chamberlain was recovering. On the afternoon of 15 August, forsaking his siesta, Churchill went to the headquarters of fighter command to watch the deploying of the squadrons against the incoming waves of aircraft. His first thought on returning to Downing Street was to say to his Private Secretary, 'Telephone Neville Chamberlain and give him the good news.' Chamberlain, moved by this consideration and longing to be back at his work, returned to duty in September partially crippled. He went to see the Prime Minister, who said how glad he was to have him back. He felt lonely and would welcome Chamberlain's counsel; he did not think they would differ, for they were complementary. Churchill made a most revealing remark, somewhat after this style: 'I am up and down. You are more steady. It is helpful to feel that my decisions are approved by your judgement.'[37] Soon it became clear that Chamberlain could not continue. He retired again to the country and died a few weeks later.

This account may help to explain a little why Churchill said in private, 'I shall never find such a colleague again',[38] and delivered a memorable speech of tribute. We have enduring cause to recall what Sir Winston used to describe as the long and splendid continuity of our island story, and to remember with affection and gratitude his own part in it. It is unnecessary and unworthy to magnify that part by denigrating others. Indeed, there is a duty to be punctiliously fair to those whom it has been fashionable to describe as 'guilty men'.

2. War and Foreign Policy: 1939–45

THE LATE LORD STRANG

I

THE questions which I shall address in this essay are these: What happens to foreign policy in war-time? How does it differ from peace-time policy? What part does foreign policy play in the war effort? How far is it affected by military developments? I shall relate these questions specifically to the example of the Second World War, and not to the history of war in general, or to war in the future.

I shall begin by briefly setting the stage.

The British people had gone willingly into the First World War, moved by an act of aggression, which they saw as a resort to violence by a power which, in contempt of international morality, was turning the familiar world upside-down. They fought from the heart, without wearing their heart upon their sleeve, but it left a deep scar upon them. One asks oneself whether they could have been expected willingly once again to risk what they would expect to be that kind of mass war – the only kind of war to which British military preparations were geared – upon so apparently limited an issue as the Rhineland, or Austria, or the Sudetenland, or indeed for anything short of a clear threat to national survival which could represent itself as a moral or ideological crusade. They may have been wrong, but that is what many people feared.

That is to put the so-called period of appeasement in one of its many perspectives. Munich, like the United States' neutrality legislation or Stalin's pact with Hitler in August 1939, may point to the fear of mass war as a determinant in foreign policy, as indeed a good deal of late-nineteenth-century history may also suggest. For the British empire, there was a danger of war from Japan as well as from Germany. But in 1939, after the occupation of Prague, which was seen as the last straw, the time came, even in so peacefully disposed a country as Great Britain, when growing fear for survival, together with consciousness of increasing strength, in a world which was again being turned upside-down by a power with an uninhibited taste for violence, overcame the fear of war; and the virtual certainty of war was faced, whatever the risks, if deterrence would not serve.

For months before, and for months after, Neville Chamberlain's three summit meetings with Hitler, many of us who were engaged in the day-to-day conduct of foreign policy had been oppressed by a sense of doom. Was there to be no position on which to stand? Were the forces of evil to prevail? Now, after March 1939, there was a lifting of the strain. In 1938, we had still had the burden of choice whether to go to war or not, in a cause outside western Europe. In 1939, the choice, by the guarantee to Poland, was already made. It was Neville Chamberlain himself who set British foreign policy on this new fully committed course in eastern Europe.

The fact of war, when it came, cast out the fear of war and served as a catalyst for foreign policy. Foreign policy was now enfranchised and at liberty to define and pursue its objectives without the old paralysing inhibitions. We could now bend all our effort for one purpose, namely to survive and maintain our position in a better ordered world. We should still have to bow to military necessity, as when in 1940 the Japanese made us temporarily close the Burma road into China. But we could work at full stretch under what was at times a terrible exhilaration, under what Churchill called the 'tonic element of mortal danger'.[1] By 1940, we were at one of the cross-roads of our history. What could the Foreign Office do? They could try to keep their heads, hold to their professional traditions, and apply heart and mind with perseverence to identify the forces that might be called in to weigh in our favour. Sir Llewellyn Woodward, in his book on *British Foreign Policy in the Second World War*, has told what he found in the documents:

A historian, reading the Foreign Office papers of this time, is struck by the way in which, without minimising the extreme gravity of the situation, the negotiations undertaken by the Foreign Office or by the Ambassadors abroad express confidence in ultimate victory. . . . The calmness of tone and manner of the Foreign Office papers in the weeks of extreme danger is almost ironical.[2]

In point of policy, the Foreign Office came well out of Sir Llewellyn's searching scrutiny. And as to the technique of war-time diplomacy, one may point to de Gaulle's wry description of what it meant to be in London at the receiving end of a concerted assault by the serried ranks of Mr Churchill's administration, or Lord Templewood's account of the way in which he welded his embassy team in Madrid into a fighting instrument.[3] As to material conditions of work, little need be said. We laboured behind shattered and boarded windows. We took our turn at fire-watching. On winter days in 1940 and 1941 we worked successfully at highest possible speed in order to let subordinate staff get away before the nightly bombardment started. There was a wide redeployment of staff. Officers came home from missions in enemy and occupied countries. We brought officers back from retirement. New people were recruited from industry, commerce, banking and the universities. We had to send staff, including some of our best men, to new war-time ministries and agencies. These recruits helped to integrate the new departments into the highly-organised Whitehall machine, and to keep the interest of the Foreign Office in view.

Great ambassadorial posts – Washington, Madrid, Moscow, Paris after the liberation – were filled by prominent men from outside the Service. Ministers of the Crown, with wide discretion in political matters, reporting to the Prime Minister through the Foreign Office, were appointed to stand as political advisers beside allied Commanders-in-Chief in the Middle East, North Africa and South-East Asia. The new tasks called for redeployment. What were the new tasks?

British foreign policy in the Second World War had three main objectives. The first was, in negotiation with neutral and non-belligerent powers, to attract these to the allied side, to deter them from joining the enemy, and to secure that they should afford the maximum of resources and facilities to the allied cause and the minimum to the enemy. The second was, in concert with the allied powers, to contribute to the organisation and successful direction of the war effort. The third objective, of a different character, was, in negotiation with allied powers, to deal with the war-time and possibly post-hostility political consequences of military operations, and, in the longer term, to define war aims and to make plans for the post-war settlement. These long-term aims and plans were mooted, almost as an act of faith, while the issue of the war was still in grave doubt. The Russians, in particular, brought forward far-reaching territorial claims and proposals before the end of 1941.

How were these objectives pursued?

Owing to enemy conquests in Europe, the range of operation in foreign affairs was geographically restricted; but, being linked now with the war effort, foreign policy was, in point of substance, widely extended; in point of objective, it was sharply concentrated; and in point of quality, it had a new intensity.

Thus, the Foreign Office in London had to watch, from the broad point of view of policy, the operations of new departments and agencies like the Ministry of Economic Warfare in the sphere of blockade, and the Ministry of Information, the Political Warfare Executive and the European Service of the BBC, in the sphere of propaganda.

The Political Warfare Executive, which controlled the operations of the BBC, came directly under the Foreign Office, but the Ministries of Economic Warfare and of Information had their own ministers, who were independent of the Foreign Secretary. However, in spite of lapses and disputes, the co-ordination of policy on economic and political warfare was, on the whole as time went on, smoothly effected. With the Special Operations Executive, on the other hand, which also had a minister separate from the Foreign Secretary, with a responsibility in the sphere of subversion overseas, but subject to policy direction from the Foreign Office, relations were less happy; and difficulties were more frequent, for example as to the support afforded by the Executive to communist-controlled resistance groups in Greece.

Then again, in Washington, after the United States became a belligerent, HM ambassador, Lord Halifax, held a watching brief, from the broad political point of view, over numerous British economic organisations; they, reporting directly to their own departments in London and working under the immediate control of the British Supply Council in North America, were represented on combined Anglo-American Boards such as the Raw Materials Board, the Shipping Adjustment Board, the Munitions Assignment Board and the Production and Resources Board.

This is not the place to comment on Anglo-American economic co-operation during the war; but an American historian has judged that 'by rationalising production not only within but between the two national economies, the dependence on the United States, which Britain had already been compelled to accept, was increased still further; and American officials came to exercise a potential stranglehold on the whole British economy'.[4]

The ambassador was also involved in the various British financial missions to Washington, including those of Lord Keynes; in the difficulties that arose over the use of lend–lease materials for British exports; and over the bearing of the lend–lease agreement on imperial preferences, and in the difficult Anglo-American conversations about oil-reserves in the Middle East. It was indeed in the economic field that some of his most successful negotiation was accomplished.[5] Still in the economic sphere, the Foreign Office had a part to play in international conferences on post-war economic questions, such as the Bretton Woods Conference on international financial arrangements and the Hot Springs Conference on food supplies. At these and at other similar war-time conferences in America, the influence of the United States was predominant.

We may now take a brief synoptical view of the various postures in which we found ourselves as the war went on.

From the outbreak of war in September 1939 until the defeat of the West in June 1940, the main effort in foreign policy was directed to transactions with the neutrals, aimed against what was judged to be a precariously balanced German economy; these were less contentious than they had been in the First World War. In the lonely and critical days from June 1940 until the German attack on the Soviet Union in June 1941 we had to pursue in an acute and almost exclusive form the diplomacy of survival, with little power to pursue the blockade. From June 1941, when for the first time a major war on land began to be fought betwen Germany and Russia, and in which our assistance to Russia greatly increased the already heavy strain on our naval and mercantile resources, until Pearl Harbor and the German declaration of war against the United States in December 1941, the crucial questions would be how far the United States could help us and whether the issue of the Russo-German war would be to strengthen or weaken Germany. After December 1941, in close co-operation with the United States, but in growing subordination to Washington, with the assurance that America was in full heart in the war, we could, in spite of early disasters, have good hope of ultimate victory. The shape of the post-war world had become a matter of prime importance, both as to the place which Great Britain would occupy in it, and as to the international organisation by which peace might be made secure. As Eden was to put it later: 'Before, we had believed in the end but never seen the means, now both were clear.' 'So', Churchill said, more exuberantly, 'So we had won after all.'[6]

For the first two-and-a-quarter years of the war, while the United States was neutral, the problems facing the Foreign Office in relation to Washington were, in presence of a still widely isolationist and suspicious US public, to convince the American administration that Britain would survive, if supported; to secure US acquiescence in and, especially after June 1941, co-operation with British blockade measures; to obtain the maximum of un-neutral American material assistance; to align the two countries upon common policies for the post-war world; and, finally, to hope ardently for the United States to enter the war.

By December 1941 these aspirations had been met. By November 1940 it was recognised in high US military quarters that US security depended largely on the fate of Great Britain. In January 1941, during his epoch-making visit to England, Harry Hopkins had assured Churchill: 'The President is determined that we shall win the war together. . . . At all costs and by all means he will carry you through.'[7] There followed the

President's ingenious, revolutionary device of lend–lease, two months later, and the policy of 'all aid short of war'; for these, the Prime Minister's monumental letter to the President of 8 December 1940[8] must be given credit as one of the decisive diplomatic acts of the war.

Then in August 1941 there was the joint statement of objectives known as the Atlantic Charter in which the President and the Prime Minister, at their first war-time meeting, spoke, as indeed the Prime Minister had already spoken on 22 June, of the 'final destruction of Nazi Germany'. We ought never to forget what the President and his associates did for us, in his own difficult domestic situation, before the United States was brought into the war.

As for the other neutrals and non-belligerents, the main objectives were to delay a declaration of war by Italy; to persuade the Soviet Union to limit the leak in the blockade and not to enter into closer economic arrangements with Germany; to try to counter the growing menace from Japan; to restrain the Government of Unoccupied France at Vichy from closer collaboration with Germany, and, in particular, from surrendering the fleet; to bring Turkey into the war on the allied side – an objective which, pressed by Churchill with persistence from 1943 onwards, failed of achievement until February 1945. We also aimed to persuade General Franco to keep the Germans out of Spain, to refrain from interfering with our North African operation, to restrict supplies of wolfram to Germany and to increase supplies to ourselves. We also needed to make corresponding (although they proved less favourable) arrangements about wolfram with Portugal, and to negotiate facilities for convoy protection in the Azores for British and, under cover of these, for US armed forces; to contest, by methods of economic warfare, for the trade of Sweden, Switzerland and Turkey; and jointly with the Russians to extort facilities in Persia, later to be exploited by the Americans as a supply route for Russia, and to force a Persian declaration of war – a military rather than a diplomatic operation.

Of the diplomatic operations, the most fruitful were those in Spain and Portugal. The success of the troublesome and at times dramatic negotiations with Spain, the non-belligerent ally of the Axis, and with Portugal, the non-belligerent friend of

Great Britain, owed much to the skill with which they were conducted. But they were facilitated also by brightening military prospects, and by the understanding which both Iberian countries had of allied sea-power, of the extent to which we could, if we would, bring pressure to bear, particularly on Spain, by withholding vital supplies of wheat and oil, and of the fact that their Atlantic islands were in jeopardy. In his *Memoirs*, the United States Secretary of State, Cordell Hull, proudly enumerates eighteen favourable concrete results of the negotiations with Spain.[9] In the negotiations with Portugal about the Azores in 1943, on the strength of ancient ties of alliance, it was the British and not the Americans who played the hand. In general, the Americans, once they were in the war, took a harsher line with neutrals and non-belligerents, other than Vichy France, than we did. In April 1944, Cordell Hull declared that the time for giving way to neutrals had passed.

France, Spain and North Africa, taken together as a stage for war-time diplomatic action by the two sides, offer a fascinating field for study.

With allies, in the early months of the war, the concern of the Foreign Office was mainly with France. France had entered the war reluctantly, under pressure from London. She had tried to divert military operations to theatres other than French territory. Lacking fighting spirit and adequate leadership, she had suffered defeat. In June 1940, the Prime Minister (now Mr Churchill) through the ambassador (Sir Ronald Campbell) tried in vain to persuade the French government in Bordeaux to decline an armistice, to transfer the administration to North Africa and to fight on from there, and to sail the fleet to ports safe from the Germans. These melancholy transactions show how powerless are mere words to reverse a settled national trend reinforced by decisive military argument. The last desperate throw in this futile but necessary diplomatic operation was the offer of Anglo-French union, an illustration of the shifts to which diplomacy can be reduced by military disaster.

After General de Gaulle had launched his appeal from London in that month, and brought France back into the war, it became evident that here was a man with a sense of history, a wide-ranging mind, sombre eloquence and a resolute spirit. There was the point of pride, the point of honour, the point of dignity and the point of burning faith in the future of France. The Foreign Office at once recognised the significance of de Gaulle. From the time of his establishment in London, through his turbulent sojourn in Algiers, down to the time when he entered a liberated Paris and duly became the head of a recognised Provisional Government, they fostered the Free French movement, accorded it progressive degrees of recognition, and bore with what patience and understanding they could the storms that he let loose upon them. This was, above all, Eden's policy. The Prime Minister too had at once seen what de Gaulle meant. But facing for long years the disasters of war, he could not bear with as much patience as Eden did the readiness of the general, with his small military contribution, to place his conception of the status of France above the broad interest of the allied war plans. Nor could he allow his relationship with President Roosevelt to be too deeply disturbed by differences as to the way in which the general should be treated.

It must always be a matter for question why President Roosevelt and the Secretary of State, Cordell Hull, and so many of the officials of the State Department, in contradistinction to a strong body of United States public opinion, nourished a bitter personal animosity against the general. There was in Washington a tenderness for the better elements of the shabby Vichy regime. There was an ill-founded belief that Vichy could be tempted to limit or reduce collaboration with Germany by a liberal policy of food supply for unoccupied France through an already yawning gap in the blockade. The State Department and the US Board of Economic Warfare were indeed in sharp dispute about the former's liberal supply policy for the benefit of Weygand in North Africa, which even the Department's apologist, Professor Langer, admits was 'a major hole in the British blockade'.[10]

For the Americans de Gaulle was a disturbing element with doubtful political intentions, who had grown up in London and was looked on as a British puppet. For Eden, he was a leader with 'a great and resounding name in France'.[11] In American eyes he stood in the way of a relaxation of tension between London and Vichy, and tended to drive Vichy nearer to Berlin. They would afford him military supplies if he would use them in the allied interest; but they would not countenance his political ambitions. More than once they thought of breaking with him entirely.

In the spring of 1944, Admiral Leahy, the former United States ambassador at Vichy, was still advising Roosevelt that Pétain, not de Gaulle, was the man to rally the French after the landing.[12] It was only very late, towards the end of October 1944, well after General Eisenhower and even Cordell Hull had seen that de Gaulle had to be established in liberated territory, that Roosevelt reluctantly, with the Prime Minister, acquiesced in the recognition of de Gaulle's administration as the French Provisional Government. Even at Yalta, some months later, as Hopkins records, Churchill and Eden had to fight like tigers for France.[13] Roosevelt still did not seem to want a strong France.

Still on the point of relations with allies, no small part of the attention of the Foreign Office was devoted to the affairs of the recognised governments of European occupied countries, established in exile in London or in Cairo: Poland, Czechoslovakia, Norway, the Netherlands, Belgium, Yugoslavia and Greece; the organisation of their armed forces, the conditions for their return, their post-war interests, and their contacts with their home-lands. This is a wide-ranging story, which I can do no more than mention here.

As when the United States was neutral, so also – indeed more so – when the United States became a belligerent, our foreign policy was decisively influenced by our relations with Washington; and, in the Far East in particular, the United States in practice took over responsibility.

What has been called the density of contact between the British and American governments over a wide range in the military and economic spheres, on the basis of the so-called 'common-law alliance', had gone far beyond normal diplomatic relations long before the United States came into the war. This found no parallel in the sphere of foreign policy proper. In war-time Washington there was no standing body corresponding to the Combined Chiefs of Staff or to the Combined Boards set up in Washington to deal with the production and allocation of resources. This may have been a disadvantage; but probably not. The truth seems to be that while there can be a combined strategy and a combined supply policy, all of which deal with the concrete use of men and materials, there cannot so well be a combined foreign policy, an identical way of treating each current problem as it arises, since the foreign policy of a state will be based upon the whole history, tradition, interest and outlook of that state; and no two states can have identical interests and outlook. It would seem that contacts between states on political matters can in the nature of things be best maintained through the well-tried machinery of diplomacy, supplemented by ministerial meetings, which can bring the national outlook into focus on every problem that presents itself. However well the United States and Great Britain might in the end agree upon the steps necessary to carry on the war, there were differences of political outlook between the two governments which emerged from time to time to cloud even the confident relationship between the President and the Prime Minister. For the President, Churchill's concern for the maintenance of the British empire, his supposed anxiety to maintain a balance of power in Europe in the British interest as against the Soviet Union, even his devotion to the institution of monarchy, were all in a tradition opposed to that of the United States. There was also the pragmatic British approach with a preference for specific agreements based on considerations of power, as contrasted with the American leaning towards the declaration of general benevolent principles of world-wide scope. At the Arcadia Conference in Washington in December 1941 and January 1942, which was the first meeting between the Prime Minister and the President after Pearl Harbor, and for which the Prime Minister wrote one of his epoch-making papers, the US representatives were warned: 'Never absent from British minds are their post-war interests, commercial and military. We should likewise safeguard our own eventual interests.'[14]

The Arcadia Conference, both politically and strategically, was decisive for the future. It had before it an already existing Anglo-American strategic plan, and an American 'victory program' for supplies. It laid the foundation for the Combined Chiefs of Staff, a body which General Marshall, the Chief of Staff of the United States Army, later described as 'the most complete unification of military effort ever achieved by two allied nations', but it was one which lodged the supreme direction of the war predominantly in Washington. The conference confirmed, in the new circumstances, the priority of Europe over Japan in point of strategy. It adumbrated the possibility of the later North African expedition. Politically, its main achievement was the United Nations Declaration, which for the first time arrayed the Grand Association publicly against the Axis. This has been described as 'the first post-Wilsonian fruit of active American diplomacy on the stage of world politics'.

With the entry of the United States into the war, Mr Churchill assumed an even more comprehensive and intimate place than before in the formulation and execution of our foreign policy, particularly those aspects of it related to the conduct of the war. It is generally agreed that, in normal times, foreign policy fares best when it is conducted by the Foreign Secretary in close accord with the Prime Minister. Of this, there are numerous examples in our history. But a Prime Minister, working in an extra-departmental environment in Downing Street, is not well placed to participate in the day-to-day work of the Foreign Office. The study by the Prime Minister of the daily distribution of Foreign Office telegrams and printed despatches, and of the papers which the Foreign Secretary may prepare for the Cabinet, is no adequate substitute for the Foreign Secretary's daily personal contacts with foreign ambassadors or for the stream of paper that flows continuously over his desk from all quarters of the world, calling for assessment and decision in the light of analyses and recommendations submitted by his professional advisers. Surveying mankind from China to Peru he can acquire that sense of international relationships which is the prime requisite in a Foreign Minister, that ability to see each event in what he will recognise as its own international environment. A Prime Minister will not normally possess this expertise. This would suggest that in the ordinary run of business Prime Ministers will do best not to try to take over but to rely on broad suggestions for action, while, if they will, keenly questioning the Foreign Secretary upon his lines of policy, and working hand in hand with him. Some Prime Ministers have sought to remedy this disability by having their own advisers on foreign policy, drawn from outside the Foreign Office. Both Lloyd George and Neville Chamberlain resorted to this practice in what must be admitted to be a less fully developed way than, for example, that of the

Kennedy regime in Washington. It cannot be said that in either case the result was of benefit to our foreign policy.

However, even under stress of war, none of this arose between Churchill and Eden. The two, as Eden said, worked hand in hand. Herbert Morrison has remarked that they were like father and son. In 1940 Churchill said to Eden, whom he later designated his successor: 'We shall work this war together.' As Sir Llewellyn Woodward has written: 'Mr Churchill's collaboration with Mr Eden was so frank and sagacious, and his own temperament so little inclined to backstairs methods that there was never any question of what might be called a "double" foreign policy.'[15]

Before the war, Neville Chamberlain, as Prime Minister, had taken one part, but one part only, of foreign affairs – namely, our relations with the European dictators – into his powerful hands, in disaccord with his Foreign Secretary, Eden, but not in general disaccord with Eden's successor, Halifax. After war had come, this overriding interest ceased. As he said at the meeting of the Cabinet on 1 September 1939, the event against which we had fought so long and earnestly had come upon us. A man who had fought so wholeheartedly and honestly for peace was not a man to fight a war all out for victory. Chamberlain's heart was not in warfare, as his whole heart had been in what he had been proud to call the policy of appeasement. The spirit in which Churchill, for his part, faced his task when he took office on 10 May 1940, was far removed from this. He went to bed that night 'impatient for the morning'; and he slept soundly, being sure that he would not fail.[16]

His zest covered the whole field, and not least that of foreign affairs, enmeshed as these were with the world-wide impact of total war. It was mirrored in the relationship, enlivened by unsleeping interference and constant argument, which he established as Minister of Defence with his chief military advisers. They, with Eden, were his cherished war-machine, who he confessed he simply couldn't replace.[17] He did not like to have new faces about him. If the Prime Minister differed from Eden, who became Foreign Secretary at the end of 1940, the difference would be argued in the open. They were in constant touch. A stream of memoranda, apposite or inapposite, flowed from No. 10 to the Foreign Office, suggesting, enquiring, warning. No little of the Foreign Secretary's time, and that of his advisers, was consumed with answering them. But this was not time wasted. The ventilation was salutary. Churchill's differences with Eden were, in general, emotional rather than rational, a matter of degree rather than of principle. In essentials the two were at one. But Churchill would often take a different view because he was absorbed in pregnant military problems, or because he did not want to fall out with the President, with whom he had larger matters to settle. A price has to be paid for alliance.

Churchill seldom moved to conferences abroad without his Foreign Secretary or a senior Foreign Office official. Exceptions were the conversations with Roosevelt at the Arcadia Conference – but he referred home the text of the United Nations Declaration; at Casablanca in January 1943 – but he consulted the Cabinet about Roosevelt's call for unconditional surrender; and at the second Quebec Conference in September 1944, where, on the advice of Lord Cherwell, he agreed with Roosevelt upon the so-called Morgenthau plan for the pastoralisation of Germany, before Eden could bring him the Cabinet's views.

Looked at in retrospect, the matters upon which the Prime Minister and Eden disagreed, and on most of which they reached an accommodation, do not bulk very large, acute though the differences may have seemed at the time. Among them were the conflicting claims of the rival guerrillas of Tito and Mihailovitch for support in Yugoslavia; Eden's greater forbearance and more positive support for de Gaulle; the need, as the Foreign Office saw it, of planning for the post-war settlement; Churchill's temporary acceptance of the Morgenthau plan for Germany; Churchill's greater tolerance for the Franco regime; and Churchill's support in opposition to both Eden and the Chiefs of Staff, for the American proposal to occupy the Azores by force.

Churchill's concern for foreign affairs derived from his own abounding and masterful personality; but it was also imposed upon him in an especial degree in war-time because he was conducting the war in concert with two heads of government who were both supreme executive authorities, as he himself was not, each with the last word on foreign policy, as on everything else. In the Cabinet, Churchill, as Prime Minister and Minister of Defence, was one minister among others, however effectively he might impose himself; and, no less than each one of his colleagues, he was answerable to Parliament. He was conscious, and proudly conscious, of his duty to the House of Commons, which more than once obliged him to repel motions of no confidence.

The correspondence between Roosevelt and Churchill will stand out in any history of the war.[18] Through all vicissitudes, they exchanged nearly 1800 high-spirited messages dealing in the frankest terms with every emergency. 'It is', the President said, 'fun to be in the same decade with you.' Two or three of Churchill's larger memoranda are imperishable historical documents. Churchill never forgot that Roosevelt was a head of state, the holder of an august office. Roosevelt for his part sustained Churchill at times of tribulation, as when Singapore or Tobruk fell. As Commander-in-Chief, Roosevelt could, and did, at times, overrule his Chiefs of Staff[19] in a way in which the British Prime Minister did not.[20] In the minds of both men, what mattered most was the solidarity of the alliance.

The two men stood in strong contrast with each other. The Prime Minister could be wayward, and perverse, but he had an essential solidity of thought, simply and grandly rooted in history and tradition. The President, a man of gay courage and of swift, creative, crusading imagination, superb politician and inspiring war-leader though he might be, was, unlike Woodrow Wilson, no thinker. Without adequate knowledge of foreign affairs himself, he too often denied himself the benefit of professional advice, preferring to rely on intimates like the ever resourceful and constructive but acutely controversial Harry Hopkins, Churchill's 'Lord Root-of-the-Matter', who, in his heyday as Lend–Lease Administrator, acted, as one British official said, almost as 'Roosevelt's own private Foreign Office'.[21] Cordell Hull had no great complaint to make about Hopkins, but he strongly resented the incursions of the Secretary of the Treasury, Henry Morgenthau. After Pearl Harbor, behaving as Commander-in-Chief rather than as President, so Cordell Hull said, Roosevelt often deliberately excluded the Secretary of State and the State Department from consultation and from participation in his conferences. In some of his conversations with Churchill, he insisted that these should be conducted without the attendance of representatives of the State Department and of the Foreign Office. Eden, as a Cabinet Minister and former Secretary of State for War, would give his opinion on military affairs: Hull, it would seem, never. Roosevelt was capable of treating grave issues with astonishing levity, or what Eden called 'cheerful fecklessness'.[22] He cherished two great illusions; one was the potentiality of Kuomintang China, and the other was the benevolence of Stalin, whom he liked to speak of as Uncle Joe.

The question may be asked how far the comparative inferiority of Britain in military power weakened the Prime Minister's hand in his transactions with the other two heads of government in the sphere of foreign affairs. One general answer may be that, since Roosevelt, as Commander-in-Chief, tended to give priority to military over political considerations, and since in military planning the Americans became more and more domiant, it was usually difficult to bring long-term political arguments effectively to bear and the disability became more marked than before in the later stages of the war. In American eyes the overriding war-aim was simply military victory. Strategy was not so much the instrument of policy as something standing on its own.

Nevertheless, the British military contribution at its high point should not be underestimated. By the spring of 1944, there was rough parity between the deployed forces of Great Britain and the United States. We bore strategic responsibility in the Middle East and the Indian Ocean area. Professor McNeill has pointed to the little-noted fact that in the Burma campaign we engaged a larger number of Japanese than were engaged in any single campaign by the Americans at any time in the war.[23]

But as the war neared its close, our relative military power waned. By the end of 1944 our proportion of forces on the western front was one half, and later, one third or less. Churchill confessed to Smuts on 3 December 1944: 'It is not so easy as it used to be for me to get things done.'[24] It became clear that, unless assisted, we should face economic collapse when the war ended: the price of our five-and-a-half-years' ordeal would then have to be paid. Churchill would sometimes have to make what he called 'terrible and even humbling submissions

... to the general aim'. And our position at the Potsdam Conference was further weakened by the change of government in July 1945.

The test of Churchill's influence would be to sample his compliances and resistances. He often had both Roosevelt and Stalin against him, not only in military strategy, but because Roosevelt thought Stalin politically a better bet than Churchill for a peaceful post-war world. But he was certainly not over-shadowed. Thus, in the political field, Churchill won his long fight with Roosevelt for the north-western zone of occupation in Germany. He sharply rebuffed Roosevelt's proposals for Indian independence or for colonial enfranchisement. He declined to go all the way with Roosevelt's policies towards Vichy and de Gaulle, or to jeopardise our tiny meat ration by joining in Cordell Hull's bitter feud with the fascist-minded regime in Buenos Aires. In the main he went his own way against Roosevelt in the sharp disputes about organisation of government in liberated Belgium and Greece. He was less successful in Italy. He made the percentage agreement with Stalin about influence in south-eastern Europe in spite of American distaste. At the Yalta Conference, he brought Roosevelt and Stalin to admit France to the Control Commission for Germany. But he failed to persuade Truman to defer the withdrawal of American and British forces to the agreed zonal boundaries in Germany pending a show-down with Stalin at a tripartite meeting.

The intensive war-time dialogue between Churchill and Roosevelt showed that, in association with a military alliance and a common strategy, there can be a substantial measure of independence in foreign policy. On the strength of our military contribution, Churchill could speak in language of greater bluntness to Roosevelt in time of war than British ministers would be likely to use to an American President in time of peace. But while the dialogue lasted, disappointed or neglected field commanders on both sides would complain either that 'Churchill has Roosevelt in his hip-pocket' or that 'Churchill is merely putty in Roosevelt's hands'.[25]

In two matters, Churchill's opinions were vindicated, but only very late: it was not until 1945 that the Americans came round to the view that he had been right in thinking it an illusion that China could play any important part in the defeat of Japan; and not until 1946 was he seen to have been correct in his warning, after the deception at Yalta, that 'Soviet Russia had become a mortal danger to the free world'. He reached the latter conclusion during what he has described as the 'deadly hiatus' in the spring of 1945[26] between the fading of Roosevelt's strength and the growth of Truman's grip, when voices of anti-British and pro-Russian sentiment were still prevalent in Washington, when the crisis with Stalin grew to a climax and when he himself was sadly conscious that he had not the power to act alone.

With Stalin, Churchill found an attitude which swung all the way from surliness and cold anger to avuncular mellowness. Stalin was at his most responsive when he was given firm news about the dates for the North African and cross-Channel operations, and at his most offensive when he thought he had been deceived about the date for the opening of the Second Front in France, or when he wrongly suspected that the western powers were negotiating for a German surrender behind his back, or once when the suicidal summer-time northern convoys were temporarily suspended, or, on one occasion, when Churchill intervened in support of the detested Polish government in London. For Stalin, Poland was the nub of the controversy between East and West. On one European question, Churchill went ahead with Stalin, in face of American objections; in Moscow in October 1944, he recognised on a percentage basis, as an interim guide for the immediate war-time future, pre-eminent Soviet influence in Romania, Bulgaria and Hungary in return for Soviet recognition of British pre-eminence in Greece, with an equal division of influence in Yugoslavia.

He defended himself to the President by saying that, in these matters, someone had to play the hand, and that was what he was doing: but he was telling the President all about it. This arrangement, which did no more than recognise the facts of military power resulting from the Soviet advance in the Balkans, and which was designed to limit Soviet expansion, did not clear up all disputes, or what Churchill had, in May 1944, called 'the brute issues', with the Soviet Union in that area; but Churchill was able, in December 1944, to remark on the loyalty with which Stalin had kept off Greece in accordance with the agreement, at the time of our military intervention to prevent an armed communist take-over in Athens, an intervention which was more than coldly regarded in Washington.

II

It was not surprising that at the three-power summit meetings at Teheran at the end of 1943 and at Yalta and Potsdam in 1945, there was growing concern with political problems. As military operations prospered on almost all fronts in 1944 and 1945, the essential differences in post-war political interests and objectives emerged. In particular, with the Soviet advances into eastern Europe and the Balkans, Soviet policy hardened and Soviet demands became more imperative. Before this, the tripartite summit meeting at Teheran, the first to be held, had delusively marked the high level of inter-allied cordiality. It had followed hard on the tripartite Conference of Foreign Ministers, again the first to be held, which met at Moscow in October and November 1943. This was the most productive of all the war-time tripartite ministerial meetings. Cordell Hull, Eden and Molotov may not have had much in common, but on this occasion they all three subordinated themselves to the task in hand more fully than the Big Three would or could do, standing on their differences and masking them with words. The momentous Declaration on General Security, proposed by Hull, pledged the parties to fight the war to the end and sketched out, in general terms, an intention to create an international organisation for the maintenance of peace and security. More concretely, the European Advisory Commission, proposed by Eden, was set up to plan for the surrender, occupation and control of Germany.

At the Teheran Conference, in spite of agreement upon a design for final victory, including the settling, even if only approximately, of a date for the cross-Channel invasion, a key point with Stalin, and the confirmation of an earlier undertaking by Stalin in due time to declare war on Japan, a key point with Roosevelt, it was not found possible to carry the Moscow political agreements any further. The political interests and objectives of the three powers, apart from their common determination to defeat the enemy and to destroy the Nazi regime, were in fact gravely divergent, and it was this that was at the root of the make-believe which marked so much of the proceedings at Yalta and Potsdam, both of them more formal affairs than the meeting at Teheran.

What Roosevelt aimed at was to get the war over as soon as possible; the early withdrawal of United States forces from Europe; the avoidance of entanglement in European political problems arising, as he conceived it, from Anglo-Soviet antagonisms and rival spheres of influence; the establishment of democratic governments in liberated and ex-enemy states, preferably non-monarchical, and the early conclusion of peace treaties with the latter; an early return to normality everywhere; and the creation of a world order for peace and security based on moral principles and democratic institutions in co-operation with the Soviet Union, under cover of which tiresome European problems could be solved, but which would nevertheless be consistent with the assertion of a dominant United States interest (or, in other words, spheres of influence) in the Far East and Latin America.

What Stalin wanted, as an immediate objective, was to be secure from Germany, and for this purpose to ensure the disarmament of Germany and to establish Soviet influence in eastern and south-eastern Europe through subservient governments internationally recognised; to have Russia's territorial demands in Europe and the Far East immediately granted; to spread Soviet influence in Turkey and Persia; to recover Russian rights in the Far East; to reconstruct the shattered economy of the Soviet Union, and for this purpose to exact massive reparations from Germany; and, underlying all this, one may infer, in the longer term, to prepare against the third war of aggression from the West, which he believed would come sooner or later, or, in the alternative, to place himself in a good posture for possible future expansion.

What weighed with Churchill was the bitter hardships of the British people; the prospect of economic collapse at home; the approaching burden of having to support the German economy; the apprehension of early American withdrawal from Europe; the fear of Soviet expansion, and the need to build up democratic Europe against it; the need for a world security organisation, with a strong regional element but without large military commitment in Europe; the need for continued American support in every field, political, military and economic; the maintenance of the British positions in the Mediterranean and in the Middle East; and the determination to preserve the British Empire.

In shaping these objectives for their foreign policies and taking their decisions within their external environments, the three statesmen were in a broad sense moved quite as much by domestic needs, by political and economic pressures, and even by the public mood, as by other considerations. This would apply perhaps more to Roosevelt in the presidential election year of 1944 than to the others. They would therefore tend to hold to the courses upon which they were set, acting under compulsions which are no less strong in war than in peace. And yet, under stress of negotiation, they would sometimes have to give way, or would sometimes cover their persisting differences under the mask of ambiguity.

Churchill faced the conference at Yalta in gloomy mood. The great allies were, he told the President, so divided; and he thought that 'the end of this war may well prove to be more disappointing than was the last'.[27]

Heads of government, burdened with the conduct of the war, meeting in unsuitable places for short periods at a time with staffs crowded together (the British and American Delegations at Yalta were together seven hundred strong), with the impediment of language and widely differing interests and outlooks, could not be expected to reach the precise, accurately expressed agreements which the best practice of diplomacy requires. It was, in fact, outside the summit conferences – as, for example, at the Foreign Ministers' Conference in Moscow in the autumn of 1943, and in the European Advisory Commission in London in 1944 and 1945 – that the professional approach brought best results, relatively free from the make-believe characteristic of scampered conferences at the highest level.

The role of what, for brevity, I have called make-believe in diplomacy is worth looking at. It has a notable part to play in war and in the aftermath of war.

It has been said, for example, that what has been called the 'solemn if unreliable assurance' in the Treaty of Utrecht that the French and Spanish crowns should never be united was put in in order to make agreement possible, not because it was thought that it would seriously bind anyone. In the same way, an American historian has suggested that the proposed Anglo-American guarantee to France after the First World War was no more than 'a way the diplomatists had to get round a difficult corner',[28] since both Wilson and Clemenceau must have known that the US Senate could not possibly accept it.

When, at a time of acute crisis in 1938, Neville Chamberlain observed of Hitler that 'here was a man who could be relied upon when he had given his word', and when he said, after the Munich meeting, that he believed that there was 'sincerity and goodwill on both sides',[29] it may be that there was more than mere naïvety in these statements. They may have been part of the very fabric of his dealings with Hitler, part of his anxiety that Hitler should not let him down, part also of his faith, that by saying them, he might help to bring Hitler not to let him down, part, that is to say, of the dynamic of negotiation.

Churchill has indeed expressly subscribed to this doctrine, which has been called the 'doctrine of therapeutic trust', in defence not of Chamberlain but of himself; the doctrine, as stated by Henry L. Stimson to President Truman, that 'the only way you can make a man trustworthy is to trust him'.[30]

Speaking in the House of Commons on 27 February 1945, on his return from Yalta, Churchill said:

> The impression I brought back from the Crimea, and from all my other contacts is that Marshal Stalin and the Soviet leaders wish to live in honourable friendship and equality with the Western democracies . . . I know of no Government which stands to its obligations, even in its own despite, more solidly than the Russian Soviet Government.[31]

Writing about this remark in retrospect, he said: 'I felt bound to proclaim my confidence in Soviet good faith in the hope of procuring it. In this I was encouraged by Stalin's behaviour about Greece.' And he went on:

> It is easy, after the Germans are beaten, to condemn those who did their best to hearten the Russian military effort. . . . What would have happened if we had quarrelled with Russia

while the Germans still had two or three hundred divisions on the fighting front? Our hopeful assumptions were soon falsified. Still they were the only ones possible at the time.[32]

We do well to remember that, absurd though it may now seem to be, for long, until he was finally reassured by Stalin, Churchill was haunted by the fear that the Russians would stop at the German frontier or make a separate peace with Hitler.

But it was at that conference at Yalta, of which Churchill had glowingly spoken, that the climax of make-believe was reached. The declaration on Poland to which, after long and acrimonious debate at seven out of the eight plenary political sessions, the three leaders subscribed, was carefully ambiguous, and not least so in the interpretation to be given to the word 'democratic'. There was to be a Polish Provisional Government of National Unity which would include democratic leaders from Poland and from Poles abroad. Mr Molotov and the British and United States ambassadors were, as a commission, to consult members of the existing Polish Provisional Government in Moscow and Poles from Poland and from abroad with a view to the reorganisation of the Provisional Government on these lines. The new Provisional Government was to hold free and unfettered elections as soon as possible on the basis of universal suffrage and secret ballot. For good measure, the three leaders also subscribed to a Declaration on Liberated Europe, proposed by the Americans, in which they undertook jointly to assist European liberated and ex-satellite states in the earliest possible establishment through free elections of governments responsive to the will of the people. In the event, all this proved to be as much of a sham as the international commission set up to carry out the Munich agreement, or the guarantee by Great Britain and France of the post-Munich boundaries of Czechoslovakia against unprovoked aggression, or Beneš's promise in 1919 that the Czechoslovak Republic would be 'a sort of Switzerland'. It was a delusion to think that there could be governments in eastern Europe which would be both democratic in the western sense and friendly to Russia. The Russians had their way, as, in the light of geographical, political and military considerations, we must now admit that they were bound to do. Churchill, correctly assessing parliamentary opinion, would have preferred to stand out – he ardently wished to save Poland from Soviet domination and had worked unceasingly with Eden to reconcile the two governments. But both he and Roosevelt gave their consent. Why did Roosevelt agree? He was in failing health. One may suppose that, with characteristic optimism, he thought that free elections might after all be held; and he so badly wanted to get the Soviet Union into the United Nations as co-pillars of the new World Order, and to maintain good feeling between the West and Russia, particularly with the prospect of a Soviet declaration of war against Japan, that he believed that he was putting first things first by subordinating the Polish question to these wider and more immediate and compelling objectives. He professed to think the differences with Stalin were largely a matter of words – which may have been true enough, if only because the words did not mean the same to the two sides. He could have had James Madison's authority for holding that, in great affairs, ambiguity can be the price of unanimity.

The word 'democratic' was again freely used in the report on the Potsdam Conference about the future administrations in Germany and in the other ex-enemy states. Bevin had the grace to admit on his return, in a speech in the House of Commons, that 'the impression we get from recent developments is that one kind of totalitarianism is being replaced by another. This is not what we understand by that very much overworked word "democracy".'[33]

Churchill also could well have recalled his fiery speech in the House of Commons on 8 December 1944, when he had castigated those who alleged that the communist guerillas whom we were suppressing in Athens were 'friends of democracy'.

Those who acquiesced in the subjection of Poland now find few to defend them. Professor McNeill has done his best for them, and on lines which Churchill had chosen:

> Reading the record in retrospect one is tempted to scorn the pious phrases which were so freely used on all sides; but it is perhaps over-hasty to do so. War-time propaganda and military co-operation had obscured the great differences between Russian and Western ideas of democracy; and it seemed imperative to many good, honest and intelligent men to

retain the common slogans in the hope that the reality of agreement might gradually grow up under the shelter of an identity of verbal formulae. Deliberately to uncover the disagreements which a common profession of faith in democracy hid might have made things worse, might even have fractured the Grand Alliance before Germany and Japan had been defeated.[34]

This is a signal example of the shifts to which war-time foreign policy can be reduced under stress of military necessity.

If, as has been suggested, make-believe in diplomacy may be defined as representing a hope that the reality of agreement may grow up under the shelter of an identity of verbal formulae, there is a famous example in a larger sphere. In revulsion from the scourge of war, a great body of the nations of the world united together at San Francisco on 26 June 1945, to nourish that hope. The Charter of the United Nations, like the Covenant of the League of Nations before it, both of them conceived in war-time, was a desperate effort, by putting words on paper, by a confident assertion and prescription of the immediately unattainable, to persuade mankind to curb and regulate its resort to the threat or use of armed force in international affairs and to live in peace as good neighbours. Here, if anywhere, in the work done at Dumbarton Oaks and at San Francisco in 1945, is an example of the good which it is trusted will come from make-believe, as we have defined it. We may ask ourselves how far that trust has so far been justified.

The next case which I choose, namely the European Advisory Commission,[35] will point a contrast with the manner in which the Big Three dealt with the future of Poland. But it will also show once again how the passions generated by total war inspire radical terms to be imposed upon the conquered, though in this case these were wisely mitigated in due course by the western powers.

As an instrument of three-power, and later, of four-power, war-time diplomacy, the EAC was *sui generis*.

It was established, on the proposal of the British Foreign Secretary, Eden, at the Moscow Conference of Foreign Ministers which met in October 1943. Its functions did not extend, as Eden would have desired, to the consideration of current European political problems of common interest connected with the war, arising before or after the cessation of hostilities. Its sphere was confined, as both the US government and the Soviet government wished, to that of post-hostilities planning and, specifically as one of its first tasks, to the preparation of armistice terms and of the machinery for their enforcement. In the nineteen months when it met at Lancaster House in London between January 1944 and August 1945 it drafted and secured the approval of governments for the terms of surrender for Gemany, a plan for the occupation of Germany, and a plan for the machinery of control in Germany, together with corresponding agreements about Austria, and terms of surrender for Bulgaria. It held twenty formal and ninety-seven informal meetings, and produced twelve protocols embodying agreements submitted for the approval of governments. The members of the Commission were usually able to assure themselves, before they signed the protocols, that their governments would in fact approve them.

The Commission was a standing body. The British member, drawn from the Foreign Office, worked full-time on the Commission. The United States and Soviet members were Mr Winant and Mr Gusev, the ambassadors in London, with all their normal work to do as well. They were joined late in 1944 by the French ambassador, M. Massigli. There was a Secretary General drawn from Whitehall, and a small staff of secretaries and interpreters. Throughout, the main impulse came from the British side. The Soviet member declined to study more than one subject at a time. At one stage, Soviet delays (we once had to wait for nine weeks for the Soviet member to agree to a meeting) provoked a protest from Eden to Molotov. The Commission was heartily disliked by President Roosevelt, who had an antipathy to the professional study of foreign affairs, and who saw, rightly, that the location of the Commission in London placed an initiative in British hands. Three times in the autumn of 1944, the President circumscribed and even at one time halted the action of the US Delegation to the Commission. The existence of the Commission was resented also by the War Department in Washington, who began by boycotting it, on the ground that the matters being treated by the Commission were matters for themselves and, in no sense, for the Department of

State, through whom the instructions to the US member were to be channelled. There was no such inter-departmental difficulty on the British side.

Nothing could be further removed from the war-time summit meetings at Teheran, Yalta and Potsdam. There was a minimum of make-believe in the agreements which we reached and put on paper. In our deliberations we were not, in general, swayed by the ebb and flow of military operations. Through all vicissitudes we worked at our plans for Germany with a single-minded endeavour, on a basis of equality, to reach common agreement. At no time did the military disparity of the United Kingdom, as compared with the two great partners, weaken the hand of the British member of the Commission. Only at three points can it be said that military operations had an impact upon the work of the Commission. The Soviet declaration of war upon Bulgaria brought the Soviet representative for the first time into the Commission's deliberations on the terms of surrender for Bulgaria. Secondly, the Soviet advance into Austria brought a note of truculence into the attitude of the Soviet representative which had been absent from his handling of German questions. Thirdly, the growing certainty that, as the war ground on longer than had at one time been expected, there would be no central German authority competent to accept terms of surrender, caused us to recast our draft into a form which would provide for the allies themselves to announce the defeat and unconditional surrender of Germany and to assume supreme authority in respect of Germany.

But, in a general way, the substance of the agreements did reflect, on the British side at any rate, a view of the current military situation and post-war possibilities. We wanted the Russians to be associated with us right up to the final defeat of Germany, and to participate with us in the post-war control of Germany. And that meant concluding agreements on equal terms.

In one respect I had an advantage over my colleagues. The British government had begun its post-war planning in good time and in an orderly way. Papers were prepared by the official Post-Hostilities Planning Sub-Committee of the Chiefs of Staff Committee, under a Foreign Office chairman, and approved by the ministerial Armistice and Post-War Committee, presided

over by the Deputy Prime Minister, Mr Attlee. As the negotiations went on, I was able to put my problems to an inter-
departmental committee, over which I presided, and which
included representatives of the Service Departments; and I
could seek instructions in person from the Ministerial Committee. The Foreign Secretary kept in close touch with all this,
but the Prime Minister did not; and there were things in the
instructions which I received which would most probably not
have commended themselves to him had he given them attention. His preoccupations were naturally directed to the conduct
of the war. The defeat of Germany lay in the distance. It was
only later that he expressed regret at some of the three-power
decisions which had been reached.

Thanks to the work of our planning staff and requisite ministerial decisions, I was able to circulate to my colleagues, at the
outset of the proceedings, comprehensive papers on all three of
the main subjects relating to Germany, namely, the terms of
surrender, the zones of occupation and the machinery of
control. At later dates, I circulated to my colleagues the
governmentally approved drafts of thirty-six directives on
various aspects of the post-hostilities treatment of Germany.
These were printed together in a handbook, but were never
considered by the Commission, in view of the American and
Russian desire to limit its competence. The US Secretary of the
Treasury, Mr Morgenthau, spoke disparagingly of these drafts;
but M. Vyshinsky had a copy of the handbook with him at
Potsdam and went out of his way to commend it.

Thus, the EAC was able to plan for the surrender, occupation
and control of Germany. It was not allowed to plan for the
post-hostilities treatment of Germany. This was left to be done,
in a superficial fashion, at the Potsdam Conference.

It was clear to us that, if we wanted our difficult negotiations
to succeed, we should have to be careful to observe equality in
our procedure. This we did, establishing relations of mutual
confidence. We worked informally. We worked in private. Our
progress, from week to week and from month to month, was
excruciatingly slow. But we edged our way towards our agreements and the sum total of our achievements was impressive.
What is more, our agreements, unlike some of those reached in
more solemn conclaves, were applied in practice, though later

in part disregarded by the Russians. I am not concerned for the moment with the substance of the agreements. They can be defended, both in the matter of the drawing of the zonal boundaries and of the access to Berlin, given the circumstances of the time. I am concerned rather to show that there can be a place in war-time for deliberate negotiation and for the careful formulation of agreements.

It may seem odd, in view of the relationship between Churchill and Roosevelt, and in view of the way in which we do things today, that I did not discuss these three main plans with my American colleague before I circulated them, or that the two governments did not confer about them before instructions were sent to me. It had, in fact, been suggested by Hopkins to Eden, in March 1943, with the President's agreement, that an Anglo-American plan for Germany should be worked out and discussed with the Russians.[36] But this was never done, and, when the EAC met, we were carrying out a tripartite agreement; we wanted to bring the Russians into the system, and this would not be facilitated by ganging up against them.

As a matter of fact, the Americans had had prior notice of the Attlee plan (as they called it) for zones of occupation, but, although they disliked it, they failed, through a characteristic defect in their administrative structure, to bring their opposition appropriately to bear. Had they done so, the German problem, and in particular the problem of Berlin, might have worn another colour. This is a complex matter, and a matter of acute controversy in the United States, but a word or two may be said here. For the United States' side of these transactions, I have drawn upon an American study of the problem.[37]

The Attlee plan, which was ultimately adopted, provided for a British zone in the north-west, an American zone in the south-west, and a Soviet zone in the east, with Berlin, lying well within the Soviet zone, under three-power control. The Soviet zone included forty per cent of the area, thirty-six per cent of the population and thirty-three per cent of the productive resources. The proposal was made generous to the Russians by our planners because they wanted to make sure of Soviet co-operation in the complete conquest and post-hostilities control of Germany, and because they wanted to limit the call to be made by the occupation upon our own resources. The boundaries of the zones would follow existing administrative boundaries. Berlin, being in the east of the country, would necessarily fall within the Soviet zone, but could not be left under the control of the Russians alone.

This plan reached the US military authorities through COSSAC, the joint Anglo-American staff in London, planning for the cross-Channel invasion. It was seen by President Roosevelt and his military advisers on 19 November 1943 on board ship on their way to the Teheran Conference. The President did not like it. He wanted the north-west zone for the United States. The Soviet zone was too big. 'The United States should have Berlin,' he said. In his light-hearted way he drew lines upon a map: a small British zone in the south-west; a much reduced Soviet zone east of a line joining the north-west corner of Bohemia with Berlin and Stettin. All the rest for the United States.

There were no representatives of the State Department on board – they had been deliberately excluded by the President. The President's views do not seem to have got through to the State Department. They do not seem to have been brought forward by the President at Teheran. At Teheran the discussion on post-war Germany ended up nowhere, and it was decided that the subject should be considered further by the EAC. At Cairo in early December, after the Teheran Conference, the American Joint Chiefs of Staff merely referred the plan back to COSSAC. So that no word of warning of the President's attitude seems to have reached HMG before the plan was circulated to the Americans and Russians in the Commission on 15 January 1944. Even then there was no reaction from the US delegation. The State Department and the War Department were deadlocked in Washington in a jurisdictional dispute, and the US ambassador was left without instructions. He seems to have had no inkling of the President's views.

A month later, on 18 February, the Soviet Delegation accepted the Attlee plan, and proposed detailed arrangements for three-powered occupation and control of Berlin.

At last, a fortnight later, the US War Department produced a plan under which the boundaries of the three occupation zones would meet at Berlin, giving each of the three powers direct access thereto. The State Department did not like it and it was sent to the US ambassador, without supporting instructions, which the War Department refused to provide. He declined to present it, since it was obvious that the Russians would not accept it, and he asked in vain for instructions. After some weeks, he sent his deputy, George Kennan, to see the President, and early in April the President gave in and said that he had no objection to accepting the proposed boundaries of the Soviet zone, since the other two delegations had agreed. All the same, he held to the demand of the United States for the north-western zone and only gave way on this, after a long struggle with the Prime Minister, at the Quebec Conference some months later.

The agreement on the zones of occupation in Germany and on the special regime for Berlin was one of the most important reached during the war, and the consequences of it bear heavily upon us today. If the American machinery of government had been in tune and alert, if the President had not pursued his policy of exclusion against the Secretary of State and his department, an approach could have been made to the Foreign Office, or indeed to Churchill himself, and the presentation of the Attlee plan to the Commission might, at any rate, have been delayed.

A whole range of questions must remain unanswered. Would it have been possible for the British and Americans to reach agreement on a modified plan? If so, would it have been possible to secure the Russians' agreement to anything differing substantially from the proposal which they did in fact accept? If there had been no three-power agreement on zones of occupation, would this have made any difference to the course of military operations on the allied and on the Soviet side? Would the western allies have pushed on to Berlin and beyond, when the Russians were temporarily halted in eastern Germany, if there had been no agreed zonal boundary for them to have to pull back to, though it is pertinent to recall that the decision to stop short was taken by General Eisenhower on military grounds? If there had been no zonal agreement when hostilities ended, would the iron curtain have come down along the final military line of demarcation, and would each side have gone its own way on its own side of the line, as indeed, when all is said and done, they have since proceeded to do? In that event, should we and the Germans have been better or worse off than we and they are now, particularly if, as is most probable, an undivided Berlin would have been on one side or the other of the demarcation line? As things have turned out, it could be speculatively if not very persuasively argued that we and the Americans might have done better to have had no EAC zonal agreement with the Russians, and to have had the maximum of Germany territory under our own occupation. But when we prepared and negotiated the EAC agreements in 1943 and 1944, we could not foresee how the military campaign would develop. Nor could we foresee how Soviet policy would evolve. It was not until some time after hostilities ended that this became increasingly plain.

We have found that, under stresss of war, and with the inextricable intermeshing of the war effort with international affairs, concern for foreign policy, and indeed the conduct of foreign policy itself, tend to be concentrated more heavily than in peace-time upon heads of government. The example which I had been quoting shows how far-reaching may be the consequences if, on a matter of prime importance, one head of government does not make full use of those best qualified to help him, and another turns a blind eye on what is going on.

The interaction between military considerations and considerations of foreign policy in war-time, between policy and strategy, is not easy to disentangle. As Eden once remarked: 'In wartime, diplomacy is strategy's twin.'[38] Ideally speaking, the rule should be that in preliminary survey policy and strategy should be kept separate; in decision, they should be brought together. But it is not often as tidy as that, and it is not always clear what is the distinction between political and military considerations. The United States' military tradition draws a sharp line between the two, and holds that military men are to dismiss other than military considerations from their minds. But since Roosevelt listened more to his Chiefs of Staff than to the State Department, the American outlook was more strongly coloured than was the British by military considerations. Still, political considerations played their part. What one must do, in examining the course of events, is to try to see where the balance lay in the decisions that were reached. Here are a few dogmatic judgments, in a sphere where I cannot claim special knowledge.

The basic British decisions to give the guarantee to Poland in March 1939, to conclude the Anglo-Polish treaty in August, and to go to war on behalf of Poland in September, were predominantly political decisions, somewhat sustained by growing military confidence, but marked by grave military hazard. Predominantly political also was the decision not to come to terms with Hitler after the conquest of Poland in 1939 or after the collapse of France in 1940. So indeed was Churchill's declaration of assistance to the Soviet Union in June 1941. The British decision to send forces to Greece to meet the German attack in March 1941 was a political decision taken with the support of a firm local military judgment that it had 'a reasonable fighting chance'.[39] The crucial American decision to give the war against Germany priority over the war against Japan was reached on compelling military grounds against the trend of public sentiment. The decision to invade North Africa in 1942 was taken by the two heads of government on grounds both political and military, against the advice of the US Joint Chiefs of Staff, on what General Eisenhower described as 'the blackest day in history',[40] an opinion which he later fully recanted. Eisenhower's decision to make a deal with arch-collaborator Admiral Darlan at Algiers in 1942, which raised a storm in Anglo-American relations, but which Stalin on grounds of *realpolitik* approved, and his decision not to press the allied advance in Europe to Berlin and Prague in 1945, which Stalin naturally warmly applauded, were both reached on local military grounds. The decision to defer the cross-Channel invasion until 1944 was a sound military judgment, taken by the two heads of government on the basis of British thinking and in opposition to US military opinion. An example of a military operation dictated predominantly by political considerations was the British intervention against the communists in Greece at the end of 1944, which was frowned on by the Americans. Another was the American general Mark Clark's militarily ill-judged decision to drive on to Rome in disregard of General Alexander's instructions; he would probably have got to Rome sooner if he had obeyed them. An example of a military operation rejected on political grounds was the American proposal, supported by Churchill, to occupy the Azores by force. The upshot seems to be that where there was conflict between political and military considerations, military considerations usually prevailed.

Some general conclusions may be drawn about the place of foreign policy in war-time as shown in the Second World War. There is nothing startling about them:

1. In total war, as then fought, foreign policy was closely integrated with the war effort.

2. In point of substance, it was widely extended; in point of objective, sharply concentrated; in point of quality, it had a new intensity.

3. In pursuit of the war effort there might be a conflict between military and political considerations in which usually, but not always, military considerations prevailed.

4. The presence or absence of immediately applicable military power would govern the outcome of diplomatic action.

5. As the war proceeded favourably for the allies, there was increasing concern with post-war political plans: in respect of general security, these tended to be utopian; and, in so far as they concerned the terms to be imposed on the enemy, such terms would, in the context of total war, be of exemplary severity.

6. There was a tendency for the major issues of foreign policy to be handled by heads of government rather than by Foreign Secretaries.

7. This favoured the entry of an element of make-believe into the results of their personal meetings.

8. More specifically; while a common strategy is consistent with a measure of independence in foreign policy, Churchill's position, throughout the war, made it wise for him to trim his diplomatic sails to his relations with Roosevelt in the overriding interest of military operations.

9. As the Soviet campaign proceeded successfully, the Soviet attitude to the allies hardened, and their political demands became more imperative.

I close with a footnote or epilogue on the war-time relations between the western powers and the Soviet Union. If we review war-time relations with Russia, several high-points stand out.

The negotiations on the eve of war had shown that Great Britain and France were ready to contemplate an alliance with the Soviet Union against Germany, but these foundered on the rock of apprehended Soviet expansion in eastern Europe. Churchill's declaration of assistance to the Soviet Union in June 1941, and the Anglo-Soviet treaties of July 1941 and May 1942, made clear that, in spite of all, we accepted the Soviet Union as a full ally against Germany. The British proposals in the EAC early in 1944 for the occupation and control of Germany demonstrated that we contemplated an equal place in the containment of Germany for the Soviet Union. The 'percentage agreement' between Churchill and Stalin in the autumn of 1944 was evidence that we feared Soviet expansion in eastern Europe and the Balkans, but hoped to make the best of it by limiting it to areas where Soviet military power was predominant. The 'brute issue' with the Soviet Union emerged in the starkest form in regard to Poland, where the Soviet Union was able to make good its will. The war-time recognition by the western powers of Soviet territorial claims in Europe and the Far East, in breach of the Atlantic Charter, represented a victory for *realpolitik* over principle. Notwithstanding all this, it continued to be firm western policy to try to build a world-order by bringing the Soviet Union, even at heavy cost, into the United Nations.

What became clear, as the war went on, but had generally been discounted at the beginning, was that Stalin had created a power of world-scale, more solid and dynamic than might have been expected to emerge under a Tsarist or any other regime.

The western powers had not seen the need, or had not been willing to face the need, to try to halt that power in eastern Europe. They had not attempted to force a withdrawal when they had the strength, but not the will, to do so; probably this was not practicable. It is with that power that the western powers have therefore had to try to find a way of coexistence. There has been a good deal of unrealistic talk about our having won the war against Germany and lost the peace to the Soviet Union. To try to win the peace in that sense would have meant risking a new war, and that no one was willing to do. The fear of total war resumed its role as a determinant in foreign policy.

3. Operation Bracelet: Churchill in Moscow, 1942

GRAHAM ROSS

CHURCHILL's first visit to Moscow in August 1942 has attracted little attention from historians, certainly much less than his second visit in October 1944. The records of the 1942 conference are admittedly of no great bulk, and at first sight the story seems clear enough. Churchill had to tell Stalin that there would be no Anglo-American invasion of France in 1942 and had to persuade him instead of the virtues of an attack on French North Africa. In this he succeeded and a relationship of sorts was established between the two men. There is, however, a good deal more to be said on two different yet related themes: the role of various individuals during the Moscow meeting and its place in the evolution of war-time Anglo-Soviet relations. During his talks with Stalin Churchill made certain proposals for helping Russia. The attempt to implement these was to illustrate not only some of the difficulties·that Britain faced in dealing with the Soviet Union but also the growing weight of the United States in the diplomatic relations of the allies. In the first half of 1942 the full impact of American entry into the war had still to be felt. But one can see distinct signs that, in dealing with Moscow, London would more and more have to look over its shoulder at Washington.

Controversy over the 1942 meeting first appeared with the publication of Lord Moran's *Winston Churchill: the Struggle for Survival* in 1966. Churchill's doctor (who in 1942 was still Sir Charles Wilson) depicts the meeting with Stalin as coming close to disaster. Upset by Stalin's rudeness, Churchill was prepared to leave Moscow without signing a joint communiqué. This would have been equivalent to admitting publicly to a disagreement with Russia at a critical moment in the war. From such folly he was only saved by the intervention of the British ambassador in Moscow, Sir Archibald Clark Kerr – later Lord Inverchapel. Clark Kerr in turn was persuaded to act by Moran himself. This was not the picture that Churchill had painted; indeed his own account scarcely mentions either man.[1]

Moran's unflattering view of Churchill provoked a counterattack in the shape of a collection of essays by people who had worked with Churchill during the war.[2] They tended to criticise Moran's portrait of Churchill rather than deal with specific episodes in detail. Only Sir Leslie Rowan, Private Secretary to Churchill at the time, said much about the Moscow meeting. Although admitting Churchill's annoyance he argued that the latter had acted out of calculation rather than ill-temper. But Rowan neither challenged Moran's version of events nor commented on Clark Kerr's role. After this flurry of excitement interest in the 1942 conference disappeared. Yet to the recollections of various participants we can add a good deal of material scattered through the files of the Public Record Office. For example, there is a manuscript letter from Cadogan to Eden written in Cairo almost immediately after the conference, and, perhaps most important, there is a lengthy account by Clark Kerr himself. This was written in diary form and survives in his highly individual script. (He always wrote with a quill pen unless forced to do otherwise.) It does not appear to have been later amended. There is, therefore, ample evidence for pursuing the course of events in Moscow.[3]

Churchill's decision to meet Stalin in person was the result of various developments in the first half of 1942 in British domestic politics, in the strategic position of the allies and in relations with Russia. After Pearl Harbor Britain found herself facing a series of military disasters of which the loss of Singapore in February 1942 and of Tobruk in June were the worst. On the face of it Churchill's government survived these shocks remarkably well, winning a vote of confidence on 29 January by 464 to 1. In February the government was reconstructed and absorbed what some regarded as the potential threat of Cripps.

In July a motion of no confidence was defeated by 476 votes to 25. But these massive majorities were in a sense illusory. They could not completely conceal a feeling of unease inside and outside Parliament. To bring down Churchill would be a considerable shock to public opinion. In any case there was no obvious alternative who could hope to command general support. Much of the criticism of the government had been ill-focused and badly presented. Yet there were some warning signs. A *Times* leader of 1 July pointed out that deeds, not words, were the key to public confidence. An *Economist* leader of 14 July was somewhat sharper. Entitled 'The other Mr. Churchill', it asked what the Prime Minister would have done had he been in opposition at the time of Singapore and Tobruk.[4]

So, Churchill's position was a disagreeable one and if the government could not produce a victory, at the very least it needed to avoid further defeats. In the Middle East Churchill could push and prod and reorganise. But he could do little directly to help the Soviet Union – and it was here that a new threat appeared by the end of July with the development of the German offensive in southern Russia. The government would clearly be open to serious criticism if it appeared to stand by and do nothing. On 15 July Harold Nicolson wrote in his diary: 'I very much fear that Churchill's own position will not survive a Russian defeat.'[5] On 22 July *The Times* put it more obliquely: 'Those who watch and wait are well aware that another adverse turn of the wheel would have its instant if unpredictable consequences here.' By 27 July the Cabinet was noting that the military situation in Russia was undoubtedly serious.[6]

Relations with Russia had moved by fits and starts since the German attack of 22 June 1941. In September the Harriman–Beaverbrook mission had produced an agreement on supplies to Russia, but this very agreement introduced what was to be a persistent and acrimonious argument over convoys to north Russia. General Ismay had accompanied the mission with the intention of discussing strategic matters, but nothing came of this. Beaverbrook apparently thought it better to keep off the subject and when he did suggest talks between the British and Soviet General Staffs Stalin did not respond.[7]

Then came Eden's visit to Moscow in December 1941. This improved the atmosphere but also raised the question of Soviet territorial claims and how these would affect a possible Anglo-Soviet treaty. Such a treaty was indeed signed on 26 May 1942 and without reference to territorial questions. This could be counted a British success but it had been a near thing. To gain the treaty Eden had come close to admitting the Soviet claim to the Baltic states despite American hostility and doubts among the government's supporters.[8] One Foreign Office official was later to take the view that Britain was in practice committed on this issue.[9] Signature of the treaty, however, enabled Eden to tell the Cabinet that relations with the Soviet Union were now on a different and satisfactory footing and Churchill to declare that the situation was transformed.[10]

This might be so, but there remained doubts on the British side about Russian intentions. Writing from Washington to Churchill on 11 January 1942 Halifax said:

> I am frightened of Stalin one day getting a good offer from Hitler which he wouldn't trust, but which if he didn't feel sure of us he would be tempted to use as a time-gatherer.[11]

Within the Foreign Office Sir Orme Sargent produced a long minute dated 5 February in which he speculated on what might happen if the Russians succeeded in pushing the Germans back to their starting point in 1941. He suggested that the Russians might be content to achieve this much and no more. This led him to emphasise the need for a treaty and at the very least for an improvement in relations with the Soviet Union. Commenting on 7 February Cadogan wrote that if Russia regained the 1941 line: 'I should be very much afraid of being double-crossed by Stalin. That I regard as the great danger.' Eden on 8 February drew the conclusion that it was necessary to come to terms with Stalin. 'This may not prevent him double-crossing us but it will at least remove pretexts.'[12] Despite these fears the Foreign Office discounted the many rumours circulating in early 1942 about Soviet–German contacts.[13] Indeed, it remained anxious to promote further discussions on strategy. In March there were suggestions for another supply mission to Moscow which would also give an opportunity to discuss strategy. Eden tried the idea on Harriman and Hopkins in April but Roosevelt did not like it.[14]

With the success of the German summer offensive, doubts reappeared about Soviet intentions. If the military position became desperate would the temptation to seek accommodation with Germany become too great? This was a shift of emphasis from the speculations of February about what Russia would do in a favourable military position but it produced equal if not greater gloom. On 22 July Sir Orme Sargent thought that if Stalin got a generous offer he might be prepared to risk 'an immediate though uncertain truce'. Cadogan thought Hitler was unlikely to offer generous terms but if he did, 'I should be distinctly apprehensive'.[15] Consultation with Moscow was thus continuing on an uncertain and *ad hoc* basis at a time when Russia's military situation was worsening. Moreover, during his visits to Britain in May and June Molotov had made clear that the Soviet Union rated the promise of a Second Front more highly than the signing of a treaty of alliance. However much the British might resent the communiqué issued at the conclusion of Molotov's talks with Roosevelt, the damage had been done. Despite the reservations which Churchill put to Molotov, the Russians treated the communiqué as a definite promise of a Second Front in 1942.[16]

Soviet pressure for a Second Front was one of the first problems that confronted Clark Kerr when he arrived in Russia in March. Cripps had become increasingly unhappy and frustrated as ambassador, feeling that his own government was ignoring him. During Eden's visit to Moscow it was agreed that he should be replaced by a career diplomat. Clark Kerr had served in China since 1938, where he had made a considerable success and impressed Cripps himself when the latter visited China in 1940. Indeed, Cripps suggested him for the Russian post, but this was not decisive in the appointment. Eden and Cadogan already had him in mind.[17] Clark Kerr was an unusual, not to say idiosyncratic, personality. Thomas Barman, who first met him in Stockholm and later worked with him in Moscow, wrote:

Clark Kerr was temperamental to a degree; highly sensitive; unorthodox; unusually perceptive; and by no means popular with his colleagues, some of whom suspected him of holding heretical views on a variety of subjects.[18]

Clark Kerr seems to have quickly made a better impression on the Russians than the ascetic and teetotal Cripps. But this could not by itself remove difficulties over substantive issues of policy. In June Molotov was at some pains to remind Clark Kerr 'that the test of the treaty lay in a Second Front and that we and the Americans must understand this'. Subsequently Molotov retreated somewhat admitting that British reservations had been made clear to him.[19] But failure to help Russia could have embarrassing consequences for the coalition government, to say nothing of the effect in the Soviet Union. Yet at almost the same time Churchill was trying to convince the Americans of the dangers of a premature attack on France. During July he persuaded a reluctant Marshall and Hopkins to abandon a cross-Channel operation in favour of an attack on French North Africa. This he could regard as a success, but Stalin would have to be told that, whatever he chose to make of the Washington communiqué, there would be no Second Front in 1942. The news would need to be conveyed carefully. Stalin had reacted sharply to a hint that the Second Front might be postponed. Roosevelt agreed on 29 July that the matter would require delicate handling but was not inclined to tell Stalin too much about Anglo-American plans.[20]

A face-to-face meeting with Stalin might seem the logical answer and one that would appeal to Churchill's temperament. The idea of a meeting had come up in a different context during Churchill's visit to the United States in June. The Czech Foreign Minister, Masaryk, was also in America at the time and he suggested to a member of the British Embassy staff that Churchill ought to meet Stalin to confirm the co-operation envisaged by the Anglo-Soviet treaty. Halifax wrote to Churchill on 20 June passing on this suggestion. The Prime Minister made no comment on the letter but he subsequently referred at least once to the possibility of meeting Stalin.[21] Apart from this there is no direct evidence on how much he thought about the idea during July. There was an argument going on with the Russians about convoys but Churchill was also much concerned about developments in the Middle East. By the end of the month he was determined to go out himself to examine the performance of the Eighth Army on the spot, and the code name 'Bracelet' originally applied to this trip only.

There is just a hint in a minute of 27 July that he had a meeting with Stalin in mind: 'no approach should be made to the Russians until I am in a position to address Premier Stalin personally'.[22] This could of course refer simply to an intended approach by letter. Be that as it may, it was a telegram from Clark Kerr which extended his proposed trip from Cairo to Moscow.

The ambassador had no knowledge of the Prime Minister's plans or of developments over the Second Front, and was therefore lucky in the timing of his message. For some time he had been brooding over the idea of a meeting between Stalin and Churchill, but had been thinking of a visit to Moscow later in the year, when the longer hours of darkness would make flying safer. Two considerations, however, led him to suggest an earlier meeting. If there was not going to be an early Second Front:

> Our reasons would have to be put to Stalin in a much clearer and more specific way than has yet been done and it seems to me there is no one who could do this as convincingly as the P.M. himself.

Secondly, the visit would be good for Russian morale at a time when the military situation was 'highly disquieting'. It was important to remove any doubts about British good faith. Although Molotov claimed to have passed on the reservations put to him in London, it looked as if he had not succeeded in fully conveying Churchill's thinking to Stalin.[23] Cadogan saw the telegram on 29 July and put the idea to Eden with obvious approval, although not thinking necessarily of an immediate meeting.[24]

On the evening of the 29th the King dined with the War Cabinet at 10 Downing Street. After the dinner Churchill held an informal Cabinet of which no record was kept and announced his intention to visit the Middle East. At this stage he had not seen Clark Kerr's telegram and is clearly wrong in claiming that he announced his intention to visit Stalin.[25] It was not until the morning of the 30th that Eden showed him Clark Kerr's telegram and Churchill seized on the idea with enthusiasm. The proposal was considered at a formal Cabinet held at 12.45 p.m., where it was agreed that there should be further discussions with one or two members of the Cabinet and Moran.[26] This meant in practice a meeting later in the afternoon between Churchill, Anderson, Cripps and Moran. The result was a foregone conclusion. Churchill was determined to make the trip and brushed aside doubts about the risks to his health.[27] There was, however, some discussion about taking Averell Harriman, who at that time was still based in London and dealing with lend–lease. As a friend of both Roosevelt and Churchill, who had already met Stalin he would be a most useful addition, not least to demonstrate Anglo-American solidarity. Cripps objected, on the somewhat surprising ground that Harriman had not made a good impression on Stalin the previous September. This may simply have been the result of Cripps's annoyance at having been ignored by the Harriman–Beaverbrook mission. Churchill did not pursue the idea at this point but told Harriman of the plan to visit Moscow at dinner the following night.[28]

The proposed visit was easily agreed with Stalin, although the latter preferred Moscow to Churchill's suggestion of Astrakan. There was some delay in contacting Roosevelt, but the President gave his approval and the Prime Minister duly set off for Cairo.[29] Harriman now succeeded in getting included in the trip. He approached Eden on 4 August saying that Roosevelt had asked him to consider himself available for any mission. Would it help if he were to join Churchill in Cairo and go on to Moscow? Eden advised him to consult Roosevelt and sent a message to Churchill the same day in favour, mainly on the grounds that this would give the talks a three-party appearance. Churchill agreed, but Roosevelt hesitated, fearing that Harriman's presence might imply lack of trust in Churchill and he only changed his mind after a direct request from the Prime Minister.[30] It is not clear whether Harriman was put up to suggesting his participation.

Much may be said about the role of chance in human affairs. An engine fault to their plane meant that Cadogan, Brooke, Wavell and Tedder were delayed at Teheran so that Churchill arrived in Moscow on the afternoon of Wednesday 12 August accompanied by Harriman and Moran among others but without his principal diplomatic and military advisers. This alarmed Cadogan and Brooke not a little. But Churchill too was apprehensive – about his ability to get on terms with Stalin.[31] Not surprisingly he seized on Clark Kerr for advice. The latter thought it would be best to give the bad news first and then make the most of the advantages of an attack on North Africa. These were the tactics which Churchill in fact employed, so he clearly paid some heed to Clark Kerr's advice. But he had already used a similar approach in his recent argument with the Americans.[32]

The first meeting with Stalin was held that same evening and Clark Kerr took notes which went into the official British record, even though Cadogan thought them 'rather subjectively' written, with too many stage asides. This did not prevent Churchill from relying on them heavily for his own version and they succeed in conveying much of the flavour of the meeting. In his own account Clark Kerr added a further touch of atmosphere:

> Each one was very restless. Stalin kept getting up and walking across the big room to a writing table into which he delved for cigarettes. These he took to bits and stuffed into his absurd curved pipe. In his turn the P.M. when he had shot a bolt got up and had a walk, pulling from his heated buttocks the seat of his trousers which had clearly stuck to them. It was indeed a warm night. There was something about this dumpy figure, plucking at his backside, which suggested immense strength but little distinction.[33]

Be that as it may, Churchill seemed to have succeeded in putting over the bad news and persuading Stalin of the virtues of operation 'Torch'. The beginnings of a good relationship had apparently been established. Clark Kerr, Harriman and Churchill himself were all very pleased at the way things had gone.[34] Nevertheless when Clark Kerr called on the Prime Minister the following morning he found him in a very bad mood which was directed mainly at the ambassador himself. Rightly or not Clark Kerr blamed this on Harriman whose sycophantic attitude towards Churchill he disliked. After lunch he had a walk with Moran who was unable to explain his patient's mood but said that Churchill had been pleased with the meeting and wanted Stalin to like him. 'That is all to the good,' Clark Kerr wrote, 'I wish that he wanted the Ambassador to like him too!'[35]

At noon on the 13th Churchill had a meeting with Molotov over which he passes rather cursorily, saying that Molotov listened amiably but contributed nothing. Here Churchill seems to have overlooked some warning signs. Molotov raised doubts about Torch; there was no absolute certainty that it would take place. The implication should have been clear. If the United States and Britain could postpone one operation could they do the same with another?[36] But Churchill ignored or misread this indication that he had perhaps not done as well as he thought in his first interview with Stalin. When the rest of the party arrived on the afternoon of the 13th they found Churchill in a confident, not to say boastful, mood. Cadogan thought he was delighted at having removed the millstone which the American communiqué had hung around his neck. The Prime Minister's good humour disappeared, however, when Tedder passed him a note that the villa was probably bugged.[37]

Clark Kerr was left out of the second meeting with Stalin on the evening of the 13th. His omission could be attributed to the arrival of Cadogan and the others but Clark Kerr himself blamed it on Churchill's bad temper and indirectly on Harriman. This is not entirely fair, since Churchill had asked Harriman the previous evening if he would mind dropping out of the next meeting. It was only at the last minute that Harriman was included, specifically at Stalin's request. Churchill fudges this point and implies that he had intended to take Harriman along from the start. Nor does he offer any explanation for Clark Kerr's absence.[38] It is possible that he did not think either man would be needed for the five points he intended to raise at the second meeting: the problem of shipping losses, growing allied air strength, post-war co-operation, Russian intentions in the Caucasus and Caspian areas and the question of Japan.[39] But Stalin seized the initiative right at the start with an *aide-mémoire* which in effect accused America and Britain of bad faith in going back on a firm promise to launch a Second Front in 1942. More than once he said that Torch did not directly concern the Soviet government. Several plans had been drawn up and then abandoned. Clearly the allies did not rate the Second Front very highly. He made various gibes about British cowardice which provoked Churchill's famous outburst about finding no ring of comradeship in what Stalin said. The speech was not translated – the embassy interpreter Dunlop was himself left speechless by Churchill's eloquence – but it impressed Stalin and the atmosphere of the meeting improved considerably. Nevertheless Churchill and Harriman were left mainly on the defensive, denying that a firm promise had been made over the Second Front.

The notes for this meeting were made by Sir Ian Jacob and lack the vividness of Clark Kerr's record of the first meeting. The strained atmosphere is not fully conveyed although the British participants all agreed that things were unpleasant. Harriman called it 'rough sledding': Cadogan found the *aide-mémoire* 'as sticky and unhelpful as could be': Jacob described the atmosphere as 'anything but harmonious'. Writing in 1969 Jacob speculated whether much of Stalin's apparent rudeness was the result of clumsy translation. Pavlov was not as proficient in English as he later became. Dunlop told Tedder the following day that Pavlov was accurate in the main but tended to turn a simple statement into a speech.[40] Churchill seems to have been taken aback by the sudden change of mood from the first meeting, although similar tactics had been employed during the Harriman–Beaverbrook mission and during Eden's visit. There is nothing to show whether he had been given a warning about this. During the meeting Harriman passed him a note:

> It was to some extent the same technique in September when I was here with Max – there is no alternative but the position you have expressed. I don't think there is much behind this. He is patient but remember he is not used to being contradicted.

Harriman maintained the same optimism in a talk with Churchill that went on until 3.30 a.m. and in reporting to Roosevelt.[41]

But Churchill was neither mollified nor reassured; on the contrary he was 'distinctly nettled' as Cadogan put it. When

Clark Kerr arrived at the Prime Minister's villa on the morning of the 14th he found everybody very uneasy. Churchill 'was like a wounded lion. He declaimed against Stalin in ponderous Gibbonesque periods.' More serious was a threat not to attend the dinner to which Stalin had invited him at the end of their stormy meeting. When Clark Kerr told him that he would have to go to the dinner there was an argument which continued during an unpleasant lunch. In the end the Prime Minister was persuaded that it would be going too far to refuse the invitation. But he was clearly going to attend in a bad frame of mind. In a message to the War Cabinet he said that he would go in the public interest. The original draft ended with the significant sentence, 'He will have to go a long way to do any good with me.' This was omitted from the final version, on whose advice is not certain. It may have been Clark Kerr since the original is among his papers.[42] On the afternoon of the 14th Cadogan saw Molotov and gave him Churchill's reply to the *aide-mémoire*. Churchill was puzzled and disheartened, said Cadogan, but Molotov refused to admit that there had been any change of attitude on Stalin's part.[43] At some point during the 14th Cadogan and Clerk Kerr also considered a message from London asking what the Russians would do with their Black Sea Fleet if they lost their remaining ports on the Caucasus coast. Did they intend to scuttle it or let it be interned by Turkey? The matter was put to the Prime Minister on either the 14th or 15th and he decided that it would be undesirable to raise the question. The decision was scarcely surprising; given Stalin's mood it would have been tactless to imply such a lack of faith in Soviet prospects.[44]

The dinner at the Kremlin on the 14th began at 9 p.m. with about 100 people present. Stalin was obviously keen to make a good impression but Churchill, in a bad mood to begin with, became annoyed at the succession of toasts which made sustained and serious conversation difficult. Even so, Tedder thought that the Prime Minister was doing his best to make the party go. Both Clark Kerr and Moran felt that the atmosphere began to improve at one stage but then something went wrong. Churchill was certainly irked by the language barrier and annoyed with the two interpreters Pavlov and Dunlop. As the dinner went on he became increasingly peevish and unresponsive to Stalin's attempts to charm him. He left at 1.30 a.m. to avoid sitting through a film and stalked out with Stalin trotting along behind him. He got Cadogan to accompany him back to the villa and burst into a tirade against the Russians. He would leave without seeing Stalin again. At the villa an argument developed about whether a communiqué should be issued. Churchill, supported by Rowan, was against issuing one and did not like the proposed Russian text. Cadogan records: 'Fortified by too much vodka I reacted strongly and a stormy session came to an end at 3 a.m.' After he had gone Churchill continued talking to Moran, complained of the language barrier and repeated that he would leave without seeing Stalin again. Let him fight his own battles.[45]

By the morning of Saturday 15 August, therefore, it looked as though the visit would end in disaster. If Churchill left without seeing Stalin again and no communiqué were issued, Anglo-Soviet relations would publicly be revealed as in a bad way. Clark Kerr was likely to stand condemned for suggesting the visit. Stalin might make another approach to Churchill before the latter left Moscow, but he was likely to be in an unreceptive frame of mind. When Clark Kerr arrived at the villa on the 15th Cadogan told him of the previous night's argument and of Churchill's determination to leave without seeing Stalin again. Would Clark Kerr try to talk him round? With everything to gain and nothing to lose Clark Kerr agreed and Cadogan went inside to persuade Churchill to talk to the ambassador. The latter, by his own account, was waiting among the raspberry bushes when he was joined by Moran, who gives a somewhat different version. He had wanted to speak to Clark Kerr but saw no chance of detaching him from Cadogan. So he wrote a letter urging that the Prime Minister be induced to see Stalin again, and gave it to John Reed, Second Secretary at the embassy, who passed it to Clark Kerr.

The latter's account makes no mention of a letter, nor does a letter from Reed to a friend, written shortly after the event. It says that Moran 'button-holed his Excellency and implored him to intervene'. This sounds more like a face-to-face conversation than a communication by letter. It would in any case have taken Moran some time to write out the reasoned arguments he describes and it is not clear whether Cadogan and

Clark Kerr had a lengthy enough conversation to make this possible. It is obvious from Clark Kerr's own account that he had taken a liking to Moran and had no reason to denigrate his part in events.[46] According to the ambassador, Moran told him of a suspicion Churchill had developed that Stalin was trying to bring down the coalition government. The Prime Minister had spoken to Moran in this vein during their conversation of the previous night. Could the ambassador see Churchill and ask him to see Stalin again? Clark Kerr doubted it. The upshot was that Moran confirmed the resolve which Clark Kerr had already made to try and talk Churchill round.

The Prime Minister came out 'lowering and sullen', but Clark Kerr persuaded him to go for a walk. Churchill stumped on ahead along a narrow path among the fir trees, turning round from time to time to glare at Clark Kerr. The latter began by saying bluntly that Churchill had gone about things the wrong way. If the visit was a failure it was his own fault. He should make allowances for the difference in the Russian approach. To this the reply was: 'The man has insulted me. From now on he must fight his own battles alone.' So Clark Kerr now argued that Stalin had not really been as insulting as Churchill made out. What had been said at the second meeting which had not been said at the first? 'But the man has insulted me. I represent a great country and I am not submissive by nature.' Now Clark Kerr tried another approach. Did Churchill realise the implications if Russia were to be defeated? We could not let her go down simply out of injured pride. 'The man thinks he can upset my government and throw me out.'

Then Churchill went on at length about his hold on the public mind and on the House of Commons. Clark Kerr retorted that his power would soon ebb if he abandoned Russia. Eventually Churchill said,

'You think it is all my fault?'
'Yes.'

There was a pause. Then Churchill asked what Clark Kerr wanted him to do. 'I told him quickly that I wanted him to send a message to Stalin to say that he would like another talk, just the two of them.' By now they were nearly back at the villa.

Churchill took Clark Kerr inside to join Cadogan. 'Alec, he says it's all my fault.' Suddenly the Prime Minister chuckled. At lunch he was transformed, holding forth on a variety of topics.[47]

This account suggests that Churchill was more concerned about his position at home than he cared to admit, although it is unclear what roused the suspicion that Stalin was trying to bring him down. By suggesting a meeting *à deux* Clark Kerr had kept himself out but this would also eliminate Harriman. The Prime Minister would, however, meet Stalin in a much better frame of mind – if the meeting could be arranged. Cadogan had originally been scheduled to meet Molotov at noon but was put off until 4 p.m. So Pavlov was summoned and asked to arrange a meeting by phone. The answer that came back consistently was that Stalin was out for a walk. Fearing to disturb Churchill's equanimity once more, Cadogan used some diplomatic licence and told him that Stalin was out of town on business. Not until 6 p.m. did an invitation come through for Churchill to meet Stalin at 7 p.m. Was Stalin simply anxious not to appear too eager? Or was there a genuine debate about how to respond? Perhaps the former, in the light of what Stalin's daughter says. She was summoned by phone during the afternoon. 'Churchill was having dinner in our apartment that night and my father had given orders that I was to be home.'[48] At some point in the day Churchill must have asked for a new interpreter and Clark Kerr scored another success by producing Arthur Herbert Birse. The latter's grandfather was a Scot who had settled in St Petersburg and Birse had himself been educated in Russia. In 1941 he was posted to the British Military Mission in Moscow as an interpreter, but had found Soviet rigidity and suspicion so frustrating that in July 1942 he applied for a transfer. This was granted but fortunately for him he was held in Moscow because of the Churchill visit.

Birse had spent the afternoon of the 15th translating at the first of two military meetings held that day. It had turned into an unproductive wrangle about the Second Front, since the Russian representatives said they had no authority to discuss air operations in the Caucasus. Having just returned to his hotel Birse received a summons by phone from Clark Kerr. The embassy interpreter was 'ill' and Birse must replace him at Churchill's talk with Stalin that night.[49] Birse had little time to be alarmed. He found Churchill cheerful but when they arrived at the Kremlin Stalin seemed glum and sulky. It was an hour or so before the atmosphere became more relaxed, and the turning-point came when Stalin invited Churchill to dinner and Molotov was brought in to join the party. At Churchill's villa Clark Kerr and Cadogan were entertaining the Pole, General Anders, who had been invited for dinner at 8.30 p.m. A phone call about 8 p.m. informed the party that Churchill would be dining with Stalin and would not be back for an hour or so. He had not appeared by midnight, when Clark Kerr abandoned the attempt to entertain Anders and went to sleep on a sofa. At 1 a.m. Cadogan was summoned to the Kremlin where he found Stalin, Molotov, and Churchill sitting at a heavily laden table. The final version of a communiqué was agreed and the party did not break up until nearly 3 a.m.[50] Birse had to make notes as best he could and he later went over them with Clark Kerr. Unfortunately, since nobody on the British side was present at all three meetings except Churchill himself we lack a unified account of the three meetings with Stalin.[51] Birse, however, had established himself as an interpreter, and was to work for both Churchill and Eden at several major conferences. When Churchill got back to the villa he was in triumphant mood. He quickly got rid of Anders and held forth on how well the meeting with Stalin had gone. A friendship had been cemented and he was glad he had come. Clark Kerr commented: 'I forgave him all his bloodiness and all his folly.' The Prime Minister was still bubbling with good spirits when he boarded his plane at 5.30 a.m.[52]

The immediate British and Russian reaction was one of satisfaction. Although the Soviet press was rather guarded Clark Kerr thought the visit had made a good impression and he found even Molotov quite expansive. Russian officials indicated to Beneš and to the Norwegian ambassador that, despite some doubts early on, they were on the whole pleased with the visit. The British were for their part impressed by Soviet determination to fight on. Stalin did not hint at any inability or unwillingness to carry on the struggle. The one sour note came from the American ambassador, Admiral Standley, who thought the visit had fallen flat. But it transpired that

Standley had resented Harriman's failure to consult him or keep him informed.[53] Nevertheless, the conference produced nothing in the way of immediate practical results. Three specific proposals which Churchill made during his visit came to nothing. Firstly, there was 'Jupiter' – the proposal for an attack on German air bases in northern Norway in order to reduce losses on the Russian convoys. This was one of Churchill's pet schemes and he got Stalin to the point of agreeing that there should be a joint Anglo-Soviet operation in November. But neither the British nor American staffs had ever been very enthusiastic about Jupiter and they became even more lukewarm as Torch drew nearer.[54] Secondly, there was 'Velvet', the plan to establish an Anglo-American air force in the Caucasus. This had been discussed inconclusively at the second military meeting on 15 August. Churchill took up the proposal with Roosevelt on 30 August but it was not until October that the President confirmed American willingness to participate. Then Stalin proved unresponsive to requests that the preliminary planning should begin. It was only on 8 November that he responded and proposed that consultations should take place in Moscow.[55] A team under Air-Marshal Drummond duly proceeded to Moscow only to find that the Russians now preferred that the planes be handed over directly to them. Neither the Air Ministry nor the Combined Chiefs of Staff liked this idea and a deadlock ensued until Drummond was summoned to see Molotov on 12 December. The latter effectively ended discussions by confirming that the Soviet government did not wish to proceed with the original proposal and wanted an equivalent number of aircraft instead. In view of their improved military position the Russians had presumably lost interest. The problem of how to obtain closer military co-operation despite Soviet suspicions remained unresolved.[56]

Nor was Churchill's third proposal any more successful, although the difficulties lingered on much longer. It is usually described as an agreement on the exchange of technical information. This was a euphemism for the exchange of information about certain types of military equipment – in practice mainly radar and signalling equipment. Discussions during Bracelet got far enough for Cadogan to produce a draft agreement and a formal exchange of notes took place on 29 September. Harriman took up the idea with the United States government but the War Department was strongly opposed to becoming involved. The Americans continued to be unco-operative and this was of considerable significance, since some of the information which Britain might be asked to supply was of American origin. Nor did the agreement produce a flow of information from the Soviet Union. She offered little and when seeking information from Britain did not invoke the agreement unless difficulty was anticipated. This made the British Service Departments increasingly unwilling to operate the agreement.

The British therefore tried to reach an agreement with the Americans about joint disclosures. But the Americans preferred to draw up a separate list of items, most of which were in fact released in October 1944. This short-circuited a lengthy British argument about the best way to proceed. By the summer of 1945 Churchill had agreed that the 1942 agreement should be allowed to lapse.[57] This particular issue raised the whole problem of how to deal with the Russians. Did one try to bargain hard or try to be reasonable? On this there was a considerable difference of view between the Foreign Office and the Service Departments which was never quite resolved. This episode illustrated how agreements reached at the highest level could prove difficult, if not impossible, to implement in practice.

On the other hand Churchill's meeting with Stalin had an important, albeit negative, effect. An open breach with the Soviet Union was avoided. Stalin now had some direct knowledge of Churchill's personality although the precise value of this is difficult to estimate. But until the Foreign Ministers meeting in Moscow in October 1943 there was no further contact between Russia and her allies at a high level and relations in the summer of 1943 were very strained indeed. The 1942 meeting may have helped considerably to ease that strain. Yet it also has to be said that Bracelet followed the pattern already set by the Harriman–Beaverbrook mission and the Eden visit. Personal contact with Stalin produced a temporary improvement in atmosphere only to be followed by fresh problems and new recriminations. The same was to happen after subsequent conferences and this helps to account for the considerable oscillations in Churchill's attitude. On the one hand he thought he had established a personal relationship with Stalin, on the other he reacted sharply to the harshness and rigidity of Soviet policy and its seeming imperviousness to outside pressure. Bracelet served a useful purpose at a critical time in the war; it also illustrated in miniature the problems which Britain had to face in dealing with Russia. Churchill and the Foreign Office never quite made up their mind on the best way to handle the Soviet Union.

4. Britain, America and the Bomb

MARGARET GOWING

In studying the history of the British atomic project I have found that every kind of history is involved in it: diplomatic history and international relations; imperial history; strategic history; constitutional and administrative history; economic history; social history; medical history; history of the press, of the universities and so forth. I used to think that perhaps the only type of history that did not come into it was religious history but now I feel that this was perhaps an important part of the whole saga.

There is one dominant theme in the history of the British atomic bomb project: that is the relationship between Britain and the United States. The unique quality of this relationship is apparent even today. Soon Britain will have to take difficult decisions about her nuclear deterrent. What Britain calls her independent deterrent is dependent on the provision of missiles, though not of nuclear warheads, from the United States; and Britain is the only foreign country to which the United States supplies them. How did this very special atomic relationship come to pass?

Understanding is impossible without going back forty years to the discovery that an atomic bomb was possible. This is a period which seems, to those well into middle age, still so near, but to those under forty so very far. It belongs to that twilight period of history – the relatively recent past – where so often myth is a substitute for historical understanding. Why then has Britain, now a very medium-sized world power and a relatively low economic performer, been over the years so determined to

possess her own nuclear deterrent? And why did she acquire
this special relationship with the United States?
Before going back to the early formative years I wish to
underline one point. I write of Britain's special relationship
with the United States but at various times Britain's atomic
relationship with America was triangular – with Canada as the
third point. The atomic story is indeed an important part of the
evolution of Canada's power status.

*

The most obvious reason why Britain was determined to have
an atomic bomb of her own after the Second World War was
that her scientists and the refugee scientists living in Britain had
invented it. Even now this is not clearly understood, for the
immense, prodigious effort of the United States Manhattan
project which made the bombs, overshadowed Britain's crucial
role, so small in terms of men and resources, so large in terms of
its consequences. This is how it happened:
The year 1939 produced one of the most extraordinary co-
incidences of all history: the discovery of the results of splitting
an atom of uranium (a material hitherto considered pretty
worthless) and the outbreak of the Second World War. It was
found that when neutrons – the fundamental particles at the
heart of the atom – bombarded an atom of uranium, not only
were various fission fragments and an immense amount of
energy released but also some spare neutrons which could fly
off and split other uranium atoms, so that a chain reaction was
possible with the release of more and more and still more
energy. Only two days before war broke out one of the greatest
physicists of the twentieth century – Niels Bohr the Dane – with
an American colleague published, for all the world to read, the
theory which gave understanding of uranium fission.[1]
Scientists in several countries had quickly seen during 1939
that uranium fission might be a source of heat and power
inconceivably greater than anything yet known. There also
seemed to be a much more slender chance that it might provide
an extraordinarily potent explosive. Was an atomic bomb to be
Hitler's secret weapon? However, by the early months of the
Second World War, scepticism had replaced the sense of

urgency, largely as a result of Bohr's paper. For this had shown that fission is far more likely to occur in certain uranium atoms – in uranium 235 – than in other uranium atoms – in uranium 238. A lump of natural uranium dug out of the earth consists of 99.3 per cent uranium 238 atoms and only 0.7 per cent of uranium 235 atoms. If a chain reaction in natural uranium is to succeed you have to slow down – or moderate – the neutrons which cause the fission so that they have a better chance of hitting the fissile U235 atoms. But if you slow the neutrons down you do not get the fantastically fast reaction you need for an explosion – for a bomb. Few scientists saw clearly that to make an atomic bomb you must have a chain reaction with fast, that is, unmoderated neutrons, and that is only possible with a lump of uranium 235. The few who did see this still dismissed atomic bombs as impracticable because it seemed an impossible task to separate the uranium 235 from the uranium 238 atoms. They are after all almost identical chemically and the difference betwen them for practical purposes is simply that a uranium 235 atom is very slightly lighter in weight.

Physicists in both Britain and America were pursuing uranium research in 1939 but they all concluded that whatever the work's long-term importance, it would not contribute to winning the war. Here, at the outset, it must be remembered that the United States was neutral in the war from September 1939 until Pearl Harbor was attacked at the end of 1941. Rather loftily, American scientists suggested in 1939 or 1940 that it would be a sheer waste of time for people busy with much more urgent matters in England to turn to uranium as a war investigation.

Then in the spring of 1940 two physicists in Birmingham, England, both of them refugees from Nazism, wrote a crucial memorandum.[2] One of them was Otto Frisch, an Austrian who was one of the discoverers of fission and who at retirement held a chair at Cambridge, and the other was Rudolf Peierls, a German theoretical physicist who at retirement held a chair at Oxford. Their memorandum showed firstly, that a lump of pure uranium 235 would give the fantastically quick chain reaction necessary for an atomic bomb. Secondly, it proposed an industrial method for separating the 235. Thirdly, it foretold the horrors which an atomic bomb would bring and saw the strategic and moral implications. A five-kilogram bomb, said Peierls and Frisch – that is, one weighing a little more than a packet of sugar – would liberate the energy of several thousand tons of dynamite and would besides cause radiations which would be fatal to living beings long after the explosion.

The Peierls–Frisch memorandum led directly to the setting-up in Britain of a committee, the Maud Committee, which was one of the most successful committees this or any other country has ever seen. It was the use of the very fast chain reaction to be obtained with uranium 235 that had led to the Maud Committee. But in the summer of 1940, before the Committee had got very far, its work was reinforced by the dramatic arrival, as France fell, of two French scientists. They came from a Paris team which had been the first to report early in 1939 the possibility of achieving a slow chain reaction in ordinary, plentiful uranium 238. Even though scientists by 1940 believed this slow reaction would be useless for a bomb, it held out to them the hope of nuclear power. The two French physicists who fled to England brought with them, in cans, the total world stock of heavy water which they had bought from Norway: this was the best known and most efficient moderator for slowing down neutrons. The Maud Committee settled the Frenchmen in Cambridge at the Cavendish Laboratory. Here, two of their colleagues predicted that in the course of slow chain reactions in ordinary, unseparated uranium a new element almost completely unknown in nature would be formed which would behave like uranium 235 and be usable for bombs. They called this element plutonium. It should be emphasised here that without the arrival of these two French scientists, the British would not have had their head start at the end of the war in building slow neutron reactors to produce both plutonium for bombs and also nuclear power. General de Gaulle never forgot this even though the British did: Britain's atomic relations with France were to conflict seriously with her relations with the United States.

The Maud Committee worked at a frantic pace, feeling the breath of their German competitors hot on their necks – justifiably so, for the German project made rather a good start in 1940 and 1941. Later it mercifully floundered. The Maud Committee reported[3] in the summer of 1941, showing lucidly and with great cogency how and why an atomic bomb was possible, certainly with uranium 235 and possibly with plutonium. The politicians now came foursquare into the business and gave the project the go-ahead. But here the big question arose. Was it possible to build the enormous plant that was required in Britain, which was being bombed and where manpower was very scarce? Would it not be better to shift the whole thing to North America? The Americans were doing a good deal of work on slow neutron reactions in ordinary uranium but although they had, early in 1941, demonstrated the fissile properties of plutonium they still thought of it as important chiefly for nuclear power. The pace was desultory and the Americans had not really grasped the point about fast reactions for bombs. Their effort till then was rather like the German effort; they made progress but did not ask the leading scientific questions. It was only when they read the brilliant Maud Report that they took the project seriously and persuaded their government to set up what became the huge Manhattan project.

It was the Maud Report that galvanised the Americans into action and there is little doubt that without the British work the Second World War would have ended before an atomic bomb was dropped. Everyone is entitled to his own views as to whether this would have been better – or worse – for mankind. But one thing is certain. Britain's conception of herself as a nuclear power was born out of this early work of her own and her refugee scientists – out of the Peierls–Frisch memorandum and the Maud Report.

When the scientists and the politicians had discussed whether the British atomic plants should be built at home or in North America opinions were divided. It was finally decided that the first pilot plants must be built in the United Kingdom, while the later full-scale plants should be built in North America – probably in Canada with help from the United States. The reluctance to shift the whole project to North America had deep roots. Several ministers felt that whoever possessed such a plant would be able to dictate terms to the rest of the world. 'However much I may trust my neighbour and depend on him,' wrote one, 'I am very much averse to putting myself completely at his mercy. I would therefore *not* press the

Americans to undertake the work.' Or, suggested another minister, an atomic bomb would present the world at last with the real possibility of an international police force. Britain and America together might be able to police and control the world. But America was after all still neutral in the war. Suppose the isolationists were triumphant there after the Second World War as they had been after the First. If the atomic bomb was a joint project developed in America, might not Britain find herself in a very embarrassing position? The British also mistrusted American secrecy and security, which seems strange in retrospect in the light of the later British atomic spy cases.

At this stage – the end of 1941 – the Americans, conscious that the British were so far ahead, wanted and proposed a joint project, jointly controlled, with the British. President Roosevelt wrote to Mr Churchill about it. But the proposal was treated very coolly. The replies were sent very tardily and were written in a most superior tone while a United States emissary was subjected to a condescending homily. The British simply wished to continue collaboration on the basis of full, mutual exchange of information.

They had, in fact, missed the bus. For the Americans had launched an all-out effort to make an atomic bomb, even before the Japanese attack on Pearl Harbor in December 1941 hurled them into the war, and totally committed them to it. From this time onwards the American project multiplied exceedingly and within six months had far outstripped the British effort in terms of resources. This growth was to surprise the British, and their failure to anticipate it was to effect profoundly Britain's own atomic efforts for the next decade or more. At the end of 1941 the British were well ahead, and had a very great deal to contribute to a combined Anglo-American project. If the two projects had at that time become closely intertwined as the Americans wished, they could not easily have been pulled apart again.

In the middle of 1942 the British saw the writing on the wall. They realised that the Americans were forging ahead very fast while they themselves had the greatest difficulty in constructing even a few pilot units of the plant for separating uranium 235. What was to be called the technological gap became for the first time painfully obvious. The British saw that they must try and get into the American project on terms of equal partnership but now for various reasons the Americans did not want them and even the exchange of information ceased. It was the Americans' turn to be dilatory and superior in answering letters and telegrams. The British were desperate, for they realised that the atomic bomb would be the key to post-war national power. They also had hopes of peaceful nuclear energy. They could not proceed on their own and they were cut off completely from all knowledge of the United States project. It was only after a great struggle that Churchill persuaded Roosevelt to sign the Quebec Agreement in 1943,[4] which gave the British the possibility of participating in the American project and led to joint exploitation and purchase of uranium supplies. The agreement had two other important provisions: one was that neither side would use the bomb against third parties without the other's consent, and the second provision was that neither country would communicate any atomic information to third parties except by mutual consent. After the Quebec Agreement was signed almost all the British physicists working on uranium 235 and fast neutron bomb calculations joined the United States project.

Meanwhile the Anglo-French slow neutron team from Cambridge had gone to Canada. They too could not proceed to the construction of a nuclear pile or reactor in war-time Britain, and it had been clear that the United States would not have them. The US government disliked the Free French and mistrusted the French component in the team while the American scientists did not much like the flamboyant French physicist who led the team. Canada, simply in order to help Britain, agreed to provide facilities and after the Quebec Agreement in 1943 the Americans underwrote this project, first at Montreal then at Chalk River in Ontario. With John Cockcroft, the English Nobel physicist, as leader of this multinational team, the project flourished. Canada, then a small nation with very limited scientific resources, became by accident of war one of the first countries to be involved in nuclear power. Her current, successful, heavy water reactors come in direct descent from the pre-war work of Juliot-Curie's Paris laboratory via the two French scientists who brought the cans of heavy water to England in 1940. Canada also took her seat at the top war-time atomic discussions of the United States and Britain, and frequently played the part of an intermediary, both then and after the war.

Britain's native project had now virtually closed down for the duration of the war and the scientists in it had emigrated to North America. They were to be found in several, but not in all, parts of the United States project: the biggest British contingent was at Los Alamos, the most secret holy of holies where the bomb was fabricated, but no British scientists were admitted to the US factories where plutonium was to be produced.

So in the end the British were the junior partners in the atomic project they had launched. Their status was apparent in the decision to drop the bombs on Japan: this was essentially an American decision although the British government's consent was duly asked for and duly given. The contribution of the British to the project was small compared with the 2000 million dollar American effort; but it was of key importance in certain crucial areas and again hastened – by a period that cannot be quantified but was probably decisive – the dropping of the bombs on Japan.

After the Quebec Agreement of August 1943, Anglo-American relations had been pretty smooth and friendly. This was primarily due to a great scientist, James Chadwick, who had discovered the neutron, had been the leading figure in the Maud Committee and was leader of the British atomic team in North America. Chadwick was slight, shy, retiring, sensitive and often ill, and indeed, Nobel prizewinner though he was, he had never been to America before 1943. He was suddenly shifted from the physics laboratories which were his natural habitat to a post of crucial importance to Britain, a post which required the highest diplomatic skill. He fulfilled his exacting task superbly well and a warm friendship grew up – improbably enough – between Chadwick and General Groves, the big and exceedingly tough army officer now in charge of the United States Manhattan project. They recognised each other as being entirely straightforward and honest.

There were one or two Anglo-American rows in this period, chiefly because of differences of view about atomic obligations to France – which the Americans absolutely refused to recognise. But soon the storms were calmed until – to mix the

metaphors – Chadwick could report to London that everything
was now 'jam and kippers'. This savoury spirit was abroad
when Churchill and Roosevelt met in September 1944 and
signed another agreement at Hyde Park[5] (the American not the
British Hyde Park) which provided that full atomic collaboration should be continued after the defeat of Japan. Mr Churchill in particular put his faith in post-war Anglo-American
control of the whole atomic business. 'Our association with the
United States', he said, 'must be permanent. I have no fear', he
added, 'that they will maltreat or cheat us.' However, none of
the atomic energy people in Washington knew of the existence
of the agreement until after Mr Roosevelt died, when they had
to ask the British to supply a copy. Some of the sceptics in the
British Embassy in Washington believed that the Americans
wanted above all a post-war American atomic monopoly and
that they profoundly mistrusted the British in anything to do
with atomic affairs. One of these sceptics gloomily reported 'the
salad is heaped in a bowl permanently smeared with the garlic
of suspicion'.

*

The two atomic bombs on Hiroshima and Nagasaki brought
the six-year-old Second World War to an abrupt end. Where
did Britain stand now? Because of the crucial importance of her
scientists' work in the war-time project there was almost no
doubt in the minds of any politicians or scientists that Britain
must go into the nuclear business straight away. At first this did
not necessarily mean atomic bombs for these were the days of
brief hopes of international control of atomic energy. Britain
wanted a flexible atomic programme, one that could be used for
weapons if need be and yet would give the kind of experience
that would help provide electricity from nuclear power in the
years ahead. A programme for building large-scale reactors to
produce plutonium was therefore agreed – a year or more before
the decision was made early in 1947 to make atomic bombs.
However, most people assumed that Britain *was* going to make
atomic bombs and indeed the engineers charged with making
plutonium had been told that it was intended for bombs which
must be made, in the vital interests of the nation, with the

utmost urgency.

Once the first decision was taken – in the greatest possible secrecy – at the beginning of 1947 to make a British bomb, an independent nuclear deterrent became a major objective of British policy. Why? Firstly, there were strategic reasons. Secondly, there were reasons of status. Thirdly, and closely connected with the other two, was the nature of Britain's relationship with the United States. To take strategic reasons first. To begin with these were of a very general kind. They were expressed in essence by an advisory committee of scientists reporting, just before the atomic bombs fell on Japan, about future technical developments in warfare. Two of these scientists were the left-wing Professors Blackett and Bernal, who later strongly opposed Britain's possession of atomic weapons. But in 1945 they concluded that the only answer they could see to an atomic bomb was 'to be prepared to use it ourselves in retaliation'. This was the kernel of the doctrine of deterrence that has governed British and western policy up to the present day.

The initial decision in 1947 to make a bomb simply emerged from a body of general assumptions. It was not a response to an immediate military threat but arose rather from a fundamentalist and instinctive feeling that Britain must possess so climacteric a weapon. It seemed, moreover, a manifestation of the scientific and technological superiority on which Britain's strength – so deficient in terms of manpower – must depend. At this time there was no United States' commitment to aid Britain or the rest of Europe in another war; and Britain could not rely on America to threaten the use of atomic bombs to serve British interests.

From 1948 when the cold war was in full swing the military threat seemed far nearer, far more specific. In 1949, with the creation of NATO, the United States was committed to Europe but doubts persisted about her readiness to threaten nuclear retaliation in other people's interests.

In the internal process of British government in the first post-war era, the only memoranda I have found which disputed the basic strategic/foreign policy reasons for Britain's bomb were written by Professor Blackett, the Nobel physicist. He had originally supported the bomb as a deterrent, but by the end of

1945 he had changed his mind and wrote to the Prime Minister urging that if Britain made bombs this would decrease rather than increase security. He feared that Britain would spend a disproportionate effort in building up a stock of bombs too small to be of military value. A year later he wrote another memorandum[6] urging a neutralist policy in atomic energy as part of a neutralist foreign and defence policy. This was partly because he had returned from a visit to America deeply disturbed about the extremely conservative United States that was emerging and by the talk there of preventive war, though he did not think such a war would be launched. Blackett's papers were closely argued and, however unacceptable their thesis, they merited at least an equally closely argued commentary, but they were met in Whitehall either with silence or by contemptuous minute writing. 'He should stick to science', wrote Mr Bevin, the Foreign Secretary.

It is sometimes supposed that there was, from the end of the war, a constant groundswell of public criticism of Britain's determination to have a nuclear deterrent but, although there was bitter debate about foreign and defence policy in these early post-war years, the atomic bomb was scarcely mentioned except by Blackett. It was only with the hydrogen bomb that opposition became vociferous: the Campaign for Nuclear Disarmament did not begin until 1957, twelve years after the war ended.

The second reason for Britain's determination to possess nuclear weapons was her faith in her great power status. I believe that Britain's crucial war-time atomic role was an important factor in obscuring from Britain her changed status in the world. The atomic bomb which symbolised America's superpower status in 1945 also seemed to symbolise Britain's very high power status. It did not seriously occur to her that Russia would explode atomic bombs first. The first Russian test in 1949, three years before the British test in 1952, was a shattering moment of truth – so much so that Sir Henry Tizard, then chief scientific adviser to the Minister of Defence, could only believe that the Russians had stolen some plutonium. But even when Russia had joined America in superpower status, Britain fell only one step below them. After all, even in 1949, other countries were only beginning to climb out of complete

prostration and devastation. Lord Cherwell, Mr Churchill's
scientific and general adviser, pointed out that if Britain did not
make atomic bombs she would 'rank with other European
nations who have to make do with conventional weapons'. 'If
we are unable to make the bomb ourselves', he wrote, 'and have
to rely entirely on the United States for this vital weapon, we
shall sink to the rank of a second-class nation, only permitted to
supply auxiliary troops, like the native levies who were allowed
small arms but not artillery.' Nuclear weapons seemed to be
the way by which a medium-sized, but technically advanced,
nation could retain great power status. It was Henry Tizard,
almost alone, who questioned this great power philosophy. He
wrote in 1949,

> We persist in regarding ourselves as a Great Power, capable
> of everything and only temporarily handicapped by econo-
> mic difficulties. We are *not* a Great Power and never will be
> again. We are a great nation but if we continue to behave like
> a Great Power we shall soon cease to be a great nation. Let us
> take warning from the fate of the Great Powers of the past and
> not burst ourselves with pride. (See Aesop's 'fable of the
> frog'.)

Britain's anxiety about her power status was closely intertwined with the third reason for her resolve to be a nuclear
power: her relationship with the United States.

Since the Churchill–Roosevelt Hyde Park agreement of 1944
(which promised post-war Anglo-American collaboration) was
unknown to the American administration, it proved worthless.
Nevertheless after the war was over at the end of 1945, the two
new leaders – Attlee, who had succeeded Churchill, and
Truman, who had succeeded Roosevelt – also agreed that there
should be full and effective atomic co-operation between their
two countries and Canada.[7] This was yet another very secret
agreement, as well it might be. For while the two leaders signed
this piece of paper, based on the hopes of a virtual monopoly of
uranium, they were also making public and lofty protestations
that the only hope for the world was to lay aside nationalist
ideas, and promote the international control of atomic energy
through the United Nations. Nevertheless it was no doubt

inevitable and even proper that the British government should want Anglo-American atomic co-operation until the United Nations millenium dawned, or as an insurance policy in case it failed to dawn.

Then in 1946 there came a terrible blow for the British. The US Congress passed an Act called the McMahon Act which *inter alia* made illegal the passing of any classified atomic information to any foreign country, including Britain: the penalties for doing so included death or life imprisonment. Senator McMahon later told British ministers that if he had known about the Anglo-American war-time relationship he would not have framed so restrictive an Act. But this was poppycock; plenty of information about Britain's role, though not about the actual Churchill–Roosevelt agreements, had been given to Congress immediately after the war.

The fact was that at this time Britain had no lobby for her atomic interests in Washington. She was squeezed between the multilaterally-minded internationalists and the isolation-minded nationalists. All this reflected a more general impatience with Britain, whose affairs now seemed of only marginal importance to the Americans – rather as they do today. Britain was the importunate poor relation, and the Americans were just not interested in the cause of her poverty, the old story of how she stood alone against the Nazis in 1940, etc. etc. Besides all this the Americans just did not like Labour, that is Socialist, governments. And so Britain counted for nothing in atomic energy provided she played the game in helping to acquire essential uranium supplies.

Whitehall believed that Britain could not launch a project without American technological and industrial collaboration. Chadwick, however, reiterated time and time again that the British knew enough to get along on their own: 'Are we so helpless', he would ask, 'that we can do nothing without the United States?' Christopher Hinton, the great engineer in charge of the industrial side of Britain's post-war project, took the same line. Indeed he said that the McMahon Act was a blessing because it would make the British think for themselves. Anglo-American atomic collaboration was not in fact of great technical concern for building atomic plants and a primitive bomb but it was of the greatest political and strategic concern to

Britain. As time went on, it was also of great importance in the technology of more advanced atomic weapons.

And so Britain refused to accept the closed door presented by the McMahon Act. Anglo-American atomic relations for ten years or more after the war were a traumatic experience for the British. They ceaselessly sought the atomic collaboration they felt to be their due but this was denied them, in spite of occasional tantalising hopes. Early in 1948 an atomic arrangement – called a *modus vivendi* – was signed[8] (yet again in great secrecy) which seemed to promise some technological collaboration. However, in practice it amounted to very little, while the promise of collaboration had been dearly bought by the British. For in this *modus vivendi* the British surrendered the clause in the war-time Quebec Agreement which said that neither country would use the atomic bomb without the other's consent – a clause which had outraged United States' Senators to whom the agreement had been confidentially revealed. This British right was surrendered shortly before the British government agreed, at the time of the Berlin airlift in 1948, that United States' bombers potentially armed with atomic bombs might be stationed in the United Kingdom. Britain now seemed to risk annihilating retaliation without even being first informed or consulted, and this danger seemed acute when the Korean War broke out in 1950 and the Americans considered the use of the atomic bomb in the Far East. It became a prime British objective to restore the right of consent, or at least consultation, which had been surrendered. So Attlee rushed to Washington and he believed that he received there a promise of prior consultation. Truman indeed gave it to him. But because Congress vehemently opposed any limitation on the President's right to authorise the use of atomic weapons, Dean Acheson, the US Secretary of State, ensured that no record of Truman's promise appeared in any American documents. In later life, Acheson spoke admiringly of Attlee's success in achieving this promise and added, 'We had to unachieve it.'[9] Only in 1952 did the British regain a right to consent before atomic bombs were used from United Kingdom bases; this did not apply to any use of bombs from overseas bases which might provoke retaliation on Britain.

Until 1949 Britain was determined to possess an independent

deterrent which must be home-grown, home-made; she simply wanted full exchange of information with the Americans, plus some scarce materials. Tizard noted that any suggestions for concentrating atomic weapon production in North America had been greeted as he put it 'with the kind of horror one would expect if one made a disrespectful remark about the King'. In late 1949 this belief was modified, partly because it was clear that the Americans' technological lead was increasing as they built up industrial factory production of more efficient weapons, while Britain was still struggling to produce one laboratory, Nagasaki-type bomb. And so the British agreed to talk with the Americans about a much deeper collaboration, a real division of effort in the production of fissile material and weapons. Britain would produce some plutonium but send it and her weapon scientists to the United States, which alone would produce weapons. The United States would provide Britain with a stockpile of atomic weapons for her own use.

The British government entered these discussions but with considerable misgivings. Ernest Bevin, Foreign Secretary, was specially unhappy about placing British capacity for atomic energy production unreservedly in American hands. If war should break out, it might be a matter of life and death for the British to use atomic weapons but their supply might be denied by American delays or disapproval of British policy. Bevin greatly feared that the Americans would control Britain's industrial development of peaceful atomic power. Britain, he said, should make *no* sacrifice which would impair her ability to deal with the United States on equal terms.

However, in the event, these 1949 talks broke down. The Americans did not want to hand over a stockpile of bombs and they wanted Britain to give up even more of her own atomic programme. The arrest early in 1950 of Klaus Fuchs, the naturalised British spy who worked at Los Alamos and then at Harwell, brought the talks to an end.

When Churchill returned to office at the end of 1951 he believed that he would get much further with the Americans than Attlee had done. He did indeed achieve, for the first time, some consultation on the American strategic air offensive, about which no information whatever had been given to the British. Moreover the earlier assurance to Attlee that attacks would not be launched from British air bases without British consent was published. But Churchill was no more successful than Attlee in securing atomic technical collaboration. The two countries continued to work in watertight compartments, wasting effort, scientific manpower and resources. The United States was exploding an atomic bomb in the Pacific as Britain exploded one in the Indian Ocean. Proper collaboration continued throughout these post-war years only in uranium procurement, where the British could help the Americans because of their influence upon governments which controlled uranium supplies.

In 1946 and early 1947 the absence of Anglo-American atomic collaboration had accompanied a general withering of the war-time special relationship between the two countries. In 1948 a general rapprochement brought a temporary thaw in atomic relations as well. But in 1949, 1950 and 1951 atomic energy was something wholly apart, something dealt with according to principles quite different from those governing the rest of foreign and defence policy. For this was a period when America and Britain had drawn very closely together again and the Americans acted with great generosity to Britain and other countries in all kinds of ways. The Anglo-American partnership was once more the mainspring of Atlantic defence. As one American journalist wrote, if the Anglo-American alliance should be dissolved, every military plan in the Pentagon would have to be torn up.

Why this discrepancy? There was in the United States what a British diplomat – who loved America deeply – called an 'ill-defined and almost unconscious feeling that atomic energy is and should remain an American monopoly, both for military and industrial purposes'. Not until the late 1950s was Anglo-American atomic collaboration at last re-established so that it became once more an integral part of the special relationship.

So the British deterrent had to be independent of the United States. It also had to be independent of Europe, even though the Marshall Plan (which gave US economic aid to Europe) and NATO were bringing the British closer to western Europe. For under the atomic agreements with the Americans, disclosure of atomic information to other countries was impossible without the Americans' consent, which was never forthcoming.

This meant in particular that Britain had to turn her back on the atomic collaboration which France desired. As I said earlier, Britain's war-time work on slow neutron reactors, first in Cambridge and then in Canada, had been directly due to the French scientists who arrived in 1940. After the war Britain had to turn down the most simple atomic requests from the French. Belgium got rather better treatment simply because the Belgian Congo was the main source of uranium in this period.

The British project was also, perforce, independent of the Commonwealth, with the exception of Canada who had belonged to the war-time partnership. By the end of the war the Canadian project was a completely joint Anglo-Canadian project, with French participation and United States' assistance. It was a far bigger outfit than Canada herself would ever have undertaken, and she wanted it to go on as a joint project. But the British wanted above all their own native project and the return of their scientists to run Harwell. The Canadians felt extremely angry and let down. Friendly exchanges continued but essentially both countries went their separate ways. It is all reminiscent of the British rejection of the United States' offer of a joint project in 1941. For later, Britain saw great advantage in a jointly planned project in Canada but Canada was no longer interested. She managed to develop her own successful reactor system based on the war-time heavy water work of Canadian, French and British scientists and companies.

*

The first phase of Britain's independent deterrence ended with the first British atomic bomb test at Monte Bello in October 1952. The explosion seemed to be a demonstration of scientific and technical competence, a proof of Britain's status as a great, if not super, power. It would surely bring Britain greater respect from the United States and greater military security. Yet when Congressmen in Washington were polled soon afterwards about atomic interchange with Britain, one of them said, 'We would be trading a horse for a rabbit.' Notwithstanding this remark, the demonstration of Britain's capacity to build most successfully, on her own, the full range of atomic plants, the bomb itself and then in 1956 Calder Hall, the first industrial-scale, land-based nuclear power plant in the world, led to the very full co-operation, especially in atomic weapons, which began in 1958 – that is to a new very special relationship.

However, a month after Monte Bello the Americans exploded their first thermonuclear device. The new arms race seemed to be of the Red Queen variety. Was Britain to join in this race in which there would be no winners, no prizes and no end save an improbable millenium on earth or a holocaust? Could Britain afford to join the race? Dare she opt out of it?

5. Nehru and the Commonwealth

SARVEPALLI GOPAL

INDIA, it has been said,[1] concerns everyone. More especially it concerns, or should concern, the people of Britain, not only because of the long historical associations but because in the more than thirty years since India's attainment of independence in 1947 there has been a continuous effort in India to sustain a close relationship between the peoples of the two countries. 'Get off our back; walk by our side'; that was the advice Mahatma Gandhi frequently gave to Richard Casey, then Governor of Bengal, in the closing years of the war.[2] The British can be said to have acted on the first part of that advice a short while later, and India's leaders were prepared to do their share in the second part and to embark on an experiment in co-operation with the former rulers. There was considerable agreement on such a policy among the thinking sections of Indian society and Jawaharlal Nehru gave articulation and effect to it.

The economic links with Britain have been important through the years since 1947; and two British scholars have recently brought home to us the advantages to both sides of not allowing these economic ties to weaken.[3] But to Nehru it was the political advantage of a continuing connection with Britain and the Commonwealth which, in the early years, was of primary concern, and Nehru believed himself to be acting in this matter to some extent, as he put it, under 'a certain pressure of circumstances'.[4] It was not just to avoid the possibility that, if Pakistan stayed in the Commonwealth and India opted out, the Commonwealth might move under the unchallenged influence of Pakistan. Wider issues were also involved. The Soviet Union was at the start aloof and distant towards India and the conflict of the government of India with the Communist Party within the country created additional barriers. So India could do little more at this time than maintain a friendly posture and look out for fresh opportunities for developing contacts with Moscow. This failure to evoke any favourable Soviet response, along with the need for financial and technological assistance, compelled close relations with the United States; and Nehru was looking for ways by which he could avoid an undue dependence upon the United States. Apart from anything else, a foreign policy of being uncommitted and exercising independence of judgment on major issues demanded this. From India's viewpoint, the United Nations, after its handling of the Kashmir issue, could not be relied upon; but the Commonwealth seemed to provide a grouping whch would both safeguard India, still shaky after partition and internal strife, and protect her from any stifling embrace of the United States. American diplomats suspected that the British themselves were encouraging an anti-American attitude in India in the years immediately after the British withdrawal.[5]

But on what basis should India remain in the Commonwealth? For nearly twenty years Nehru had led the campaign for full independence as against Dominion status, and the Constituent Assembly had resolved, at Nehru's instance, months before the final transfer of power that India should be a free and sovereign republic. Nehru had no intention of going back on this and his stand had wide support. To facilitate partition and the creation of two independent states, India and Pakistan had been declared to be Dominions. But this was, as far as India was concerned, an interim measure. India would not remain a Dominion; whether as a republic she could have a closer relationship with Britain and the Commonwealth than with other countries -- as Nehru termed it, 'some vague bond'[6] -- whether any such nexus was possible was the only issue. As Attlee continued to press the desirability of more specific forms of association, Nehru formulated his proposals. These proposals moved away from legalist issues and were based on far-reaching, even visionary, concepts. India would be a republic; but a separate statute could be enacted providing for common citizenship throughout the Commonwealth. This idea of a common citizenship probably owes much in its imaginativeness to Churchill's offer to France in 1940 and, if taken up, would have altered the nature of the Commonwealth far more than the mere admission of a republic. One has only to consider the difference to world affairs that would have been made by the peoples, say, of India, Pakistan and South Africa having common citizenship in the years after 1949. But the suggestion, frequently repeated by Nehru during the discussions, was not considered seriously by the other Prime Ministers. Attlee and his colleagues from the Dominions attached more importance to the position of the Crown. Winston Churchill was more flexible, and found a precedent in Roman history for the presence of a republic in the Commonwealth, but both Churchill and King George seem to have thought in terms of the King becoming the President of India. Krishna Menon, then India's High Commissioner in London, was as anxious as any British statesman for a continuance of the Commonwealth association. He formulated an ingenious proposal for what he termed 'dormant sovereignty', whereby India would not assert all her sovereign rights but would permit the King to exercise some of them.[7] But no such camouflages were acceptable to Nehru, who was aware of the keen sensitivity in India about any formal diminution of India's newly-gained independent status. The solution clearly lay in finding some place for the King in the Commonwealth relationship without giving the Crown a place in the Indian constitution. Nehru himself preferred the language of the Statute of Westminister, 'symbol of the free association of the members of the Commonwealth'. But finally, as a compromise, he accepted the wording which speaks of 'the King as the symbol of the free association of its independent member nations and as such the Head of the Commonwealth'. Nehru disliked the phrase 'Head of the Commonwealth' but did not think it worth while to insist on its deletion especially as Malan of South Africa had it placed on record that this designation did not imply that the King discharged any constitutional function.

Nehru's immediate hopes of the Commonwealth were not unanswered. It shored up India's stability, saved her from isolation and probably even gave India greater freedom of action. Some Asian countries outside the Commonwealth felt more confident about consultation and close relation with India merely because she was in the Commonwealth. 'We are apt', Nehru warned Jayaprakash Narayan, who was at that time a severe critic of India's decision to remain in the Commonwealth, 'to be too sure of our stability, internal and external. Taking that for granted, we proceed to endeavour to remodel the world.'[8] Gradually, as India's security seemed less threatened, her relations with the Soviet Union prospered and India shed her early apprehension of the United States, the psychological dependence on Britain correspondingly declined. But now, as India came out more into the world and Nehru began to exercise a growing personal influence in international affairs, the Commonwealth became useful to India as a multi-racial forum not just for consultation but even for joint action. It is of interest that in 1954, soon after the Geneva agreements on Indochina, Nehru sent Ho Chi-Minh, at the latter's request, a note on the working of the Commonwealth so that President Ho might consider working out some similar arrangement with France.

These advantages of the Commonwealth connection were secured by India without any compromise of independence in policy. In 1953, when the Commonwealth Prime Ministers met at the time of the Coronation, the key position was held by India's Prime Minister. It was his contacts with the Chinese government which made the Commonwealth one of the crucial junctions in world affairs. Despite Nehru's irritation with Britain's viewpoint on Kashmir, his general attitude to that country was still cordial. He disliked the recruitment of Gurkhas for the British army; but he assured Krishna Menon that he would not allow this to develop into a major issue. However, on British policy in East Africa, Nehru was outspoken. While he regretted the Mau Mau movement and the recourse by Africans to violence, he believed that, in face of British provocation, the Africans had really no alternative. 'We are all', he noted on one of the official files in 1953, 'for the multi-racial society, but I am getting a little tired of the repetition of this phrase when the African is being kicked, hounded and shot down and the average Indian [settler] prays for safety first.' Nothing, thought Nehru, that the Africans had done was as bad as the naked and brutal racial domination of the white settlers. A public speech on these lines, criticising the British government and assuring the people of Kenya of India's sympathy,[9] roused the wrath of Lord Swinton, the British Commonwealth Secretary, who deemed it to be interference with British domestic interests. Nehru replied to Swinton that racialism in Africa was a world problem on which Indians held strong opinions, and if he had not stated his views moderately and without ill will, others in India would have said much more. He had himself consistently supported India's membership of the Commonwealth and praised British policy on many matters; but his arguments would have been weakened if he had remained silent on this issue of Kenya. He rejected an official note of protest from the British government and continued to express the same views both in private to Churchill and the British ministers and to the British public in press and television interviews when he was in London in 1953; but all – it must be admitted – with no immediate effect.

However, Churchill more than any other British Conservative statesman, recognised Nehru's basic friendliness towards Britain. Though Churchill had been a diehard opponent of India's freedom, he had always been less hostile to Nehru than to the other leaders of the Indian National Congress. Nehru's criticism in 1938 of British foreign policy seems to have earned Churchill's approval, for he sent Nehru a message of good will on the eve of Nehru's visit to China in 1939. After 1947, Churchill did not allow the shadow of the past to fall on their relations, and he recognised a similar attitude in Nehru, whom he once described as a man without fear and without hate. In 1949 Smuts, then out of office in South Africa, cabled to Churchill, also out of office, how much he deplored India's continuance as a republic in the Commonwealth. Churchill cabled back to Smuts: 'When I asked myself the question, "Would I rather have them in, even on these terms, or let them go altogether?" my heart gave the answer "I want them in".'[10] When the Anglo-Egyptian treaty on the Suez base was being negotiated, Nehru in 1953, on a visit to Cairo, advised Nasser not to use harsh language against Britain even while standing firm on the issue of sovereignty, and Churchill saluted this gesture in a cable to Nehru. 'Thank you so much for your message and for the help you gave us over Egypt and Israel. Winston.'[11] Two years later, on the eve of his retirement from office, Churchill wrote again to Nehru in typical Churchill style:

> I hope you will think of the phrase 'The Light of Asia'. It seems to me that you might be able to do what no other human being could in giving India the lead, at least in the realm of thought, throughout Asia, with the freedom and dignity of the individual as the ideal rather than the Communist Party drill-book.[12]

This warmth of relations between Churchill and Nehru is worth emphasising because two of Churchill's successors, Eden and Lord Home, have spoken bitterly, and as I see it unfairly, in their memoirs of India's role in the Suez crisis. In the spring of 1956 Nehru's good will for Britain and the Eden government was almost without reserve. He agreed, at Britain's insistence, not to buy any Soviet military aircraft for the time being and promised not to take any such step in the future without informing and consulting the British government. At the Conference of Commonwealth Prime Ministers that summer, he fully agreed with Eden's analysis of the changes brought about by Khruschev in the outlook and direction of Soviet policy. Both Nehru and Eden believed that fresh opportunities for peace had been provided by the new flexibility in Soviet attitudes. This general partiality for Britain coloured Nehru's first reaction to Egypt's nationalisation of the Suez Canal. He thought that there was an element of warmongering in this action and rejected the suggestion made in India for an immediate declaration by all the Bandung countries expressing clearly their support for Egypt. So well known was Nehru's critical attitude at the start that Eden informed the foreign editor of *The Times* that he even expected Nehru's support in taking military action against Egypt.[13] But Nehru's efforts to play fair by both Britain and France and not be swept along unthinkingly by the tides of nationalism and anti-colonialism were hindered by Eden himself. The sharp reaction of the British government to the nationalisation of the canal spurred Nehru into advising Eden against any attempts at coercion; but he was more than willing to help Britain in securing a negotiated settlement. Hearing of Britain's intention to convene a conference to consider international control of the canal, Nehru suggested to Nasser that Egypt herself might take the initiative and call together all those interested to consider the international aspects of the question on the basis of Egypt's sovereignty.[14]

This advice of Nehru was rejected by Nasser; so Nehru declared his willingness to participate in the London conference even though Nasser had requested him to decline the invitation. His object in going to London, he told Nasser, would be to work for conciliatory approaches; and he added to his letter what was clearly meant to be a rebuke: 'We wish to emphasise these [conciliatory] aspects and not to support any unilateral action taken by one nation or any group of nations.'[15]

The London conference could not be expected to reach any settlement, as Egypt was not represented; and the efforts of India's delegate, Krishna Menon, were directed towards preventing any rash steps from being taken and leaving the door open for further consultations. Menon sought to persuade the western powers to negotiate with Egypt on the basis of her sovereignty. So far from functioning virtually as Egypt's spokesman, as Eden and Lord Home have since alleged, Menon had to ask Nasser to counter the growing impression that India had no influence in Cairo. But Nasser disliked Menon's compromise proposals and could not have relished the suggestion that Egypt abide by the decision of the Hague Court in the matter of barring Israeli ships from the canal. In fact, while both the British and the Egyptian governments were willing to utilise India's mediatory services if these fell in line with their own thinking, neither Britain nor Egypt was prepared to listen to Nehru's advice.

By September, as we now know, Eden was committing himself to military action. When rumours of this reached Nehru he protested to Eden against endangering whatever prospects still remained of a peaceful settlement.

In my mind and in my approach to you I do not contemplate or advocate appeasement, to which references are frequently made, but a settlement that is satisfactory and honourable. This should be fully consistent with the interests and the position and prestige of the United Kingdom, which you know are our concern as well.[16]

But Nehru still could not believe that Britain would wage war on this issue and therefore persevered with informal soundings on both sides. He pressed Britain to negotiate and he urged Egypt to be a little more co-operative. To avoid any suggestion of ganging up with Nasser, he asked Nasser not to come to Saudi Arabia when he was there and he declined to supply to Egypt bren guns and fuses for mortar bombs. Krishna Menon presented Nasser with a fresh set of proposals which the government of Britain had appeared to accept.

All these efforts were brought to an end by the military attack on Egypt, an event on which Nehru had no hesitation in taking sides. India's support for Nasser was public and unqualified; but Nehru sought to link this with efforts to bring the campaign to a speedy end and to save the Commonwealth from dissolution. He subdued the growing storm of hostility in India to Britain as well as to the Commonwealth as a whole. In his speeches and his private communications he did not criticise Britain or even the British government but only Anthony Eden; and as Mr Malcolm MacDonald, then the British High Commissioner in Delhi, has testified, Nehru was not so much indignant as bewildered at Eden's action.[17] He constantly reminded the Indian public that Eden did not symbolise the totality of British opinion. There was dissent even within the Conservative Party, while the Labour Party looked to Nehru to rescue Britain from her predicament. As Mr Callaghan said a few years ago, in British Socialist eyes 'the Commonwealth was India, Pakistan and Ghana, but mostly India'. Mr Callaghan added that Hugh Gaitskell was almost romantically dedicated to the idea of preserving Britain's links with the Commonwealth, while Nye Bevan saw India as the brown link with the emerging black nations of Africa.[18] The *Economist*, writing on 1 May 1954, was critical of the British Labour Party's attitude to Nehru, which the journal described as falling little short of canonisation. Now, in the Suez crisis, many leading members of the Labour Party turned to Nehru. 'There is, as you know,' Lord Pethick-Lawrence wrote to Nehru in November 1956, 'a great number of people here in the United Kingdom whose views are similar to yours, and we hope you will not desert us in our struggle to rescue the Commonwealth from the disgrace which our Prime Minister has put upon it.'

Such appeals strengthened Nehru's hand in withstanding the pressure within India for walking out of the Commonwealth. To all such arguments he replied that Britain had no monopoly of that association and stressed that India was working particularly closely with Canada in this crisis. In fact Nehru forced Nasser, against his wishes, to agree to Canada's participation in the international force organised to supervise the ceasefire. So, when the storm passed, the Commonwealth emerged intact. Nehru, it can be said, was not only one of the creators of the new Commonwealth; he was also, in its first major crisis, its saviour.

The misunderstanding in British official circles of Nehru's policy on Suez and their failure to appreciate his desire to help perhaps explain what seemed to Nehru a fresh note of aggressiveness in British policy on Kashmir. He warned Mr Macmillan that this might affect relations with Britain and possibly also India's continuance in the Commonwealth. Once again there was a fairly widespread feeling in India that the Commonwealth connection was hardly worth while, and Nehru had again to stand forth as almost a lone, but decisive, protagonist. At a personal level, Nehru got on better with Mr Macmillan than with any other British Prime Minister; and Mr Macmillan, who visited India, has told us that he was impressed by the very strong position in India of the British, especially business men.[19] But divergences on policy continued. When in 1958 British troops moved into Jordan following a change of government in Iraq, Nehru did not publicly criticise Britain and declined to act jointly in this matter with Yugoslavia or with Sri Lanka and Indonesia. But he privately made his disapproval clear to the British government, warned against intervention in Iraq and, as a forestalling measure, quickly recognised the new regime in that country. His criticism of the attitude of the western powers in the Congo and his insistence that the occasion of South Africa becoming a republic should be utilised to exclude her from the Commonwealth, did not please the British government; while Nehru in turn disregarded Mr Macmillan's advice not to use force to expel the Portuguese from Goa. Mr Macmillan was also unable to prevent what Eden had succeeded in doing six years earlier, the purchase by India of Soviet aircraft.

Even in the matter of India's border troubles with China, Britain's support of India was not as unhedged with restrictions as appeared at first sight. When large-scale military campaigning began in October 1962, Mr Macmillan stated promptly that whatever the Indian government wanted the British to do, that they would at once do. This offer was warmly welcomed in India, for it came alongside hesitations by some Asian countries and even suggestions by African leaders of the Commonwealth that Britain should stay aloof. But in fact Mr Macmillan attached conditions to the assistance which Britain provided. He restrained President Kennedy's enthusiasm to support India without worrying too much about Kashmir, and attempted to convert the crisis into an opportunity to wrest from Nehru a settlement of that problem.

From Suez onwards, therefore, the governments of India and Britain were hardly ever in full sympathy; and, though Nehru tried hard to keep this apart from the Commonwealth association, he was not ever again as effective in this as he had been at the time of Suez. He had moved the Commonwealth association from its traditional foundations of blood and allegiance and had helped to make it work, with considerable success, on the basis of a common will and a shared sense of values. In the seventeen years that Nehru led India and took a lead in Commonwealth counsels, that association, without developing into a third force balancing between the two parties in the 'cold war', had displayed a recognisable coherence. But such coherence was already beginning, by the time of Nehru's death, to slacken; and the inner cohesion was also weakening. The departure of South Africa has not meant the exorcism of the racial issue, and one of Nehru's last letters was to Sir Alec Douglas-Home protesting against the suggestion that Mr Ian Smith be allowed to attend the Prime Ministers' Conference. That problem is still with us in a much larger and more complicated form. In India there has been in recent years an unresisted spread of what a writer years ago in *The Round Table* termed the 'inert acceptance' view of the Commonwealth.[20] It is thought that, whatever its achievements and programmes in the economic and educational fields, and despite the Commonwealth's acquisition of a very competent secretariat, the association has lost much of its political and diplomatic significance and continues because no one is concerned to put an end to it. This is not, of course, because India's commitment to the Commonwealth was primarily a personal preference of Nehru which could not substantially outlast him, but because both India and the other members have been drawn by other interests and many of them have found other attachments. But it is still worth considering, even in the altered world context, whether the kind of functional and not merely consultative association which Nehru sought to promote has yet a role to play in the world, and whether a positive effect to resuscitate the political and diplomatic Commonwealth would have some advantage.

More important, perhaps, as well as more enduring and of continuing vitality, have been the links, which Nehru's life and work symbolised, between India and Britain, not so much between the two governments as in the fundamental areas of thought and precedent. Nehru, like so many of his generation of middle-class Indians, had his roots in two countries. As an undergraduate his mind responded, not so much to the Fabians who were so popular in the Cambridge of his day, as to William Morris. The revolt of Morris against the ugliness of industrial capitalism and its impoverished human relationships had led on to a frontal attack on class exploitation and the evils of imperialism. The life of Morris was the story of the evolution of a revolutionary, the progress from aestheticism to the basic question of class power; and Nehru would seem, in his own context, to have moved in the same direction. Nehru's moral fastidiousness reacted to the social setting in which he found himself. Even where British rule in India was concerned, Nehru was always drawing attention to its vulgarity and the coarsening and degradation that it involved to both the rulers and the ruled. So when later Nehru came to Marxism, it was to him not so much a unitary logical construction as an intellectual impulse based, to a considerable extent, on sympathy.

Marxism also, paradoxically, toned down Nehru's vehement condemnation of the British for being alien rulers in India. His quarrel now was with systems and not just with the foreigner who happened to be dominating his country. Nehru gave new emphasis to the interlinking of economics and politics, of capitalism and imperialism, and saw history not as the achievement of individuals or of nations but as the product of general impersonal forces. He did not, therefore, need to smother any longer his attachment to Britain and, though often driven to exasperation, Britain was a country with which throughout his life Nehru identified extensively in the personal sense. He told the judge on the first occasion when he was sentenced to prison, in May 1922, that he had returned from England ten years earlier as much prejudiced in favour of England and the English as it was possible for an Indian to be; and he believed that in working for India's freedom he was acting as any average Englishman uncontaminated by imperialism would have done. His autobiography, published in 1936, revealed to the West a man who thought and spoke in the language of modernity and reason, whom, unlike Gandhi, the West could understand, a man like themselves who happened to find himself on the other side. Even Nehru's Marxism was qualified by what he had derived largely from the liberalism and non-conformity of Britain, an acceptance of civil liberty as an absolute value to be safeguarded at all costs. As early as 1929, presiding for the first time over the Indian National Congress, which was an organisation with middle-class leadership and with little economic programme worth mentioning, Nehru had proclaimed that he was a socialist. He never ceased thereafter to assert that the only key to the solution of the world's problems, and of India's problems, lay in socialism, using, as he put it, the word 'not in a vague, humanitarian way but in the scientific, economic sense'. Nehru claimed in the thirties to be a full-blooded Marxist, but in fact he was always a libertarian Marxist, whose ideas of socialism encompassed at every stage a large and irreducible measure of civil liberty. A belief in democracy was the core of Nehru's socialist attitude. He rejected any mechanical view of human nature and looked forward to a socialist society which, by removing economic and social obstacles and inhibitions, would provide greater scope for individual freedom.

Acting on this conviction that one could have neither democracy nor socialism without the other, Nehru initiated as Prime Minister what appeared to be a superhuman task of constructing democratic socialism in a setting of conservative tradition and economic backwardness. The experiment was unprecedented; it could even be said to be anti-historical. For in the West liberal democracy has developed gradually, lending weight to the theory that it can endure in its clearest form only in the context of capitalist industrialisation. If such democracy is not to be 'premature', it has to be intertwined with, or perhaps only follow, considerable social and economic advance. Socialism too, in India, has to be very different in its basic approach from that known in the West. It has to be a rapid movement towards industrialisation rather than the liberation of an inc ustrial proletariat from capitalist organisation. Was Nehru attempting the impossible and, because of the British influences on his mind, seeking to transform by democratic methods a large, impoverished, deprived society into a rational, forward-looking one, based on modernisation, industrialisation and a scientific temper?

Mr Malcolm Muggeridge is representative of those who believe that Nehru undertook a task that had never a chance of success. It has seemed to Mr Muggeridge that Nehru was too British in outlook to achieve anything worth while in India. Meeting Nehru a few months before his death, Mr Muggeridge described him a 'a man of echoes and mimicry, the last Viceroy rather than the first leader of the liberated India'.[21] Curiously, Nehru himself would have agreed with a part of this verdict; for he once told Professor Galbraith that he was the last Englishman to rule over India.[22] But this did not mean that Nehru despaired of his own life's work. His plans to build socialism did not go ahead as fast and as surely as he would have liked, but he laid well the foundations of the democratic system. He ensured the precise elaboration in the constitution of the rights of the individual, and he saw to it that the courts had full authority to enforce those rights. Ignoring all conventional wisdom, Nehru gave adult suffrage to a people the large majority of whom were illiterate. He accustomed Indians to political participation through a series of free elections. Keenly conscious of the urgency of progress, he yet preferred to slow down the pace rather than brush aside resistance and incomprehension. The unquestioned leader of the Indian people, Nehru could have taken the easy course of acting by decree and ordinance; in fact he lent his personal command to building up the prestige of Parliament. Nehru took seriously his duties as leader of the House and of the Congress Legislative Party, sat through the daily question-hour and all important debates, treated the presiding officers with extreme deference, and built up parliamentary activity as an indispensable sector in India's public life. The only criticism that has been made of Nehru's endeavours in this matter of establishing parliamentary institutions and practices is that, too greatly influenced by the British example, he perhaps erred in intervening, during the making of the constitution, to secure the rejection of proportional representation, which might have been better suited to a federal system. But, on the whole, it was an unparalleled effort. The elections in India in 1977 form, in a basic sense, testimony to the lasting quality of this aspect of Nehru's work, and to the validity of Nehru's faith that parliamentary democracy will bear a transplant.

6. The British Nuclear Deterrent: Problems and Possibilities

EDWARD SPIERS

THE British nuclear deterrent has attracted considerable interest in scholarly and political circles. Several books have been written about the subject. The House of Commons Expenditure Committee has issued two reports on Polaris. A spate of articles has appeared in the academic journals, and an informative report has been published by Chatham House. Nevertheless, outstanding issues remain; especially the question of whether Britain should renew her nuclear deterrent, a question left unanswered by the recent Chatham House report.[1] The issue is here examined by reviewing the original reasons, strategic and diplomatic, which prompted Britain to seek a nuclear deterrent; by considering the relevance of these reasons in later years when Britain became a nuclear power; and, finally, by analysing the problems and possibilities which beset any decision to renew the deterrent. The historical aspect, in short, should be placed in perspective before making pronouncements about future policy.

Britain's strategic nuclear force, apart from a fleet of ageing V-bombers, comprises four nuclear-powered ballistic-missile submarines (SSBNs). Each submarine carries sixteen Polaris ballistic missiles with a maximum range of 2500 nautical miles. Each missile can deliver three separate thermo-nuclear warheads, with a yield of 200 kilotons apiece. The fleet of submarines was designed to operate over a span of twenty years. In view of the stress on the submarine hulls, it would be unwise to extend that period by more than another five years. As the four submarines were commissioned between 1967 and 1969, they cannot be expected to remain a credible deterrent system beyond the first half of the 1990s. To provide a new deterrent for the 1990s – that is, one designed, tested and produced in Britain – would take approximately thirteen years. This allows two years for the design of a new boat and an improved reactor, another year for the testing and evaluation of components, and about ten years to build five boats, two at a time, at the only remaining shipyard (Barrow) equipped to construct nuclear-powered submarines. Five boats represents the minimum number required to ensure that two submarines are always at sea and in a firing position. An alternative deterrent, based upon nuclear-powered submarines carrying cruise missiles, would number seventeen boats (to provide the same target coverage from submarines, carrying twenty-four cruise missiles apiece, about half of which could not be expected to reach their targets). This fleet would take at least as long to construct as a fleet carrying ballistic missiles.[2] In other words, if the British government wishes to replace its deterrent in the 1990s, it must decide by 1980.

This might not happen. Conceivably, Mrs Thatcher's government could simply let the issue drift until, say 1984 or 1985, and then seek to buy another deterrent from the United States. This option would be quicker and possibly cheaper. Britain could repeat the achievement of the 1960s, when the Polaris force was fully deployed within eight years of the Nassau Agreement. But problems attend delay. Britain cannot assume that the financial terms would be as propitious as those agreed at Nassau. To pay a mere five per cent over the retail cost, in lieu of expenditure upon research and development, was, in the words of Harold Macmillan, 'not a bad bargain'.[3] A similar deal would not be likely in the 1980s. Moreover, American weapon technology is designed for her own strategic purposes. The air-launched cruise missile and the Undersea Long-range Missile System (ULMS) designed to carry Trident missiles are under development in the United States. The air-launched platform of the former might prove too vulnerable for British purposes, while the 4000 mile range and additional cost of Trident I might seem excessive for Britain[4] (although the new technology of the Trident I system, which can be fitted into a submarine of ordinary size, might seem an attractive proposition at an acceptable price). The United States, in any case, might not wish to transfer weapon technology during the course of negotiations towards a third agreement in the Strategic Arms Limitations Talks (SALT), due to be completed in 1985. Although formal restrictions upon the transfer of technology have not been written into the SALT-2 agreement, a 'non-circumvention' clause has been included by which both parties agree not to circumvent the provisions of the treaty through third parties. Should the treaty be ratified by the US Senate, this clause could inhibit the policies of the American administration during the SALT-3 negotiations.[5] The British government, therefore, would be prudent to consider options other than simply relying upon the purchase of American technology in the mid-80s.

In considering the issue of renewal, the historical origins and development of the British nuclear deterrent merit review. The crude military potential of the atomic bomb was perceived by the Maud Committee, which reported in 1941. It claimed that 'no nation would care to risk being caught without a weapon of such decisive possibilities'.[6] Fearing that Germany might make her own bomb, Britain embarked upon atomic research at first alone and then, after the Quebec Agreement of August 1943, in conjunction with the United States and Canada. Britain continued her programme in the aftermath of the war, instituting a large nuclear research establishment and planning the production of fissile material – decisions which predated the breakdown of atomic collaboration between Britain and the United States in July 1946. Having inherited an evolving atomic energy programme, the Attlee government had simply sustained its development. In January 1947, the Prime Minister summoned certain Cabinet ministers to an *ad hoc* and highly secret meeting, where they resolved to make the bomb.[7]

Production of the bomb had always been an implicit outcome of the atomic energy programme. As the prospects of international control of atomic energy under the United Nations had already deteriorated by the end of 1946, the principal scientific advisers of the British government, with the exception of Professor P. M. S. Blackett, favoured the production of a British bomb.[8] Military leaders, whose beliefs in the efficacy of strategic bombardment had been reinforced by Hiroshima and Nagasaki, endorsed this advice. Indeed the Chief of the Air Staff anticipated the ministerial decision by placing the first requisition for an atomic bomb through the normal channels to the Ministry of Supply in August 1946, while the Air Ministry issued specifications to the aircraft industry for the development of a four-engine jet bomber (clearly an atomic bomber though not designated as such) on 1 January 1947.[9]

At this time the 'revolutionary' implications of the bomb upon the doctrine and technology of war were not foreseen; it was simply assumed that Britain must acquire a weapon of such devastating potential. As in the pre-war years, Britain still possessed vast overseas responsibilities and limited military capabilities. Although Britain maintained a level of defence spending in 1946 at roughly twice the inter-war average, her forces were extremely stretched by imperial commitments, duties in Palestine, involvement in Greece where a communist take-over was feared, and by contributing to the armies of occupation in Europe, Africa and the Far East.[10] Britain, moreover, was both vulnerable and isolated. Her density of population and concentrated industrial centres would have served as ideal atomic targets. The United States had not yet committed herself to Europe through the Marshall Plan and NATO; in fact she had abruptly halted lend–lease and atomic collaboration. Britain could not depend upon the United States threatening to use her atomic bomb to protect British interests. As Attlee recalled, there was always the possibility of the United States 'withdrawing and becoming isolationist once again. The manufacture of a British bomb was therefore at that stage essential to our defence.'[11]

Perceptions of status complemented these strategic concerns. By possessing nuclear weapons, Britain would affirm her status as a great power with a world-wide role and influence. Making an atomic bomb would underline Britain's tradition of leadership, and her continuing capacity in the realms of science and technology. It would serve, too, as a compensation for her lack of economic and military resources, especially her deficiency in manpower. It seemed inconceivable that Britain would not make the bomb; indeed it was a profound shock for British scientists that Russia completed her first atomic test in 1949, three years ahead of Britain. Labour and Conservative leaders felt that Britain as a great power, whose international status was reflected by her membership of the Security Council, must acquire all new major weapon systems. Unwilling to abandon their notions of Britain's status, successive governments accepted that developing 'atomic power was the price of remaining a great state'.[12]

Coupled with these aspirations was the desire to recover some influence in Washington. The Quebec Agreement of 1943, the Hyde Park Memorandum of 1944, and the Truman–Attlee–King concordat of November 1945 had contained secret provisions about trans-Atlantic co-operation on atomic energy: these were largely negated by the passage of the US Atomic Energy Act, often known as the McMahon Act, of 1946. This Act, which prohibited the disclosure of classified atomic information to any foreign country, left a threefold legacy. It reinforced British suspicions about solemn commitments given by her former war-time ally. It stung scientists and engineers, like James Chadwick and Christopher Hinton, into redoubling their efforts to produce a British bomb. Above all, it ensured that British governments would spend the next decade or more trying to restore a degree of atomic co-operation with the United States in order to reduce the cost and to increase the speed of their own atomic programme. These governments believed that Britain, by possessing her own deterrent, might recover some influence over American policy.[13] In summary, then, Britain had sought her own nuclear capability to augment her defences, to reflect her great-power status, and to restore her former collaboration with the United States.

Some scholars have questioned whether Britain achieved all or any of these objectives by deploying a nuclear deterrent. They have doubted that the possession of nuclear weapons enhanced relations with the United States; indeed British weapons conflicted with one strand in American foreign policy, namely her opposition to nuclear proliferation.[14] Any British influence upon Washington, claims Robert Osgood, should be attributed to the quality of her diplomacy, national leadership, historical image, geographical position and conventional military power. The special relationship, he adds, would have existed with or without a British deterrent, based upon mutual interest, a common culture, and harmonious personal relationships.[15]

The importance of these factors, especially the role of personal relationships and the requirements of common defence planning once Britain and the United States had become members of NATO, cannot be gainsaid. But the success of Britain's nuclear programme in the early 1950s was an additional bargaining lever. Negotiations alone had not secured any exchange of nuclear data which could be of use for military purposes. Only after Britain's first atomic test off the Monte Bello Islands in October 1952 could her diplomats and scientists argue that a pooling of nuclear information would benefit the United States. Britain had also tightened her security measures after several breaches of security in the late forties and early fifties. Two British scientists, Nunn May and Klaus Fuchs, had been convicted of espionage; while another, Bruno Pontecorvo, had defected to the Soviet Union. In 1951 Donald Maclean, a diplomat, who had had access to atomic information while serving in the British Embassy in Washington from February 1947 to September 1948, also fled to Russia. The British adoption of positive vetting procedures facilitated the resumption of Anglo-American co-operation in atomic research. The US Atomic Energy Act of 1954 permitted the sharing of data about the external characteristics of nuclear weapons, without disclosing information about their design and manufacture. After the British explosion of a thermo-nuclear device off Christmas Island, in May 1957, came the amendment of the Atomic Energy Act in the following year. From bilateral agreements of 1955 and 1959, Britain obtained privileged access to American nuclear information. Under the terms of the second accord, she could buy component parts of nuclear weapons and even weapon systems from the United States.[16] As the third nuclear power, Britain had joined the nuclear club.

A fundamental paradox was already apparent. As Britain strove for strategic independence, she was willing to become ever more dependent upon American technology. The access which Rolls-Royce secured, in 1955, to details of the liquid-fuelled engine of the Atlas missile was thought to have saved five years from the Blue Streak programme and to have reduced its cost by £400 million.[17] These savings proved illusory. Improvements in the accuracy of ballistic missiles rendered Blue Streak vulnerable to pre-emptive strikes, and costs mounted as Britain pioneered research in the hardening of underground missile silos. When the programme was cancelled, Britain acquired the option to purchase Skybolt and later the Polaris missile from the United States. Indeed the dependence went far beyond missile technology. It included details about the launching system, components of the inertial navigation system, the fire control, satellite intelligence, some of the communications equipment, testing facilities in Nevada, and even the high stress steel for the submarine hulls.[18]

American generosity reflected more than cultural ties and harmonious personal relationships. In the late fifties and early sixties, Britain still had something to offer as a major ally with shared or common interests. Britain provided bases for American bombers, Thor missiles, and later, American Polaris submarines. She supported the United States during several international crises, notably the Cuban missile crisis (1962). She preserved a presence east of Suez, so easing the strain on America's Far Eastern forces.[19] As a nuclear power, too, Britain played a leading part in the nuclear test-ban negotiations from 1958 to 1963. Coral Bell has asked the right question in respect of these talks: 'On what basis, if not that of her own possession of nuclear weapons, was Britain a member of the three power talks which concluded the test-ban treaty?'[20] Aneurin Bevan, in fact, had missed the point when he chided advocates of unilateral disarmament in the Labour Party for threatening to send 'a British Foreign Secretary . . . naked into the conference chamber'.[21] Without nuclear weapons, Britain could never have entered the conference chamber, naked or otherwise. Indeed she was involved in negotiating not only the Partial Test Ban Treaty of 1963 but also the Non-Proliferation Treaty of 1970, and sits alone with the United States and the Soviet Union in the current deliberations on a Comprehensive Test Ban Treaty (France and China having excluded themselves).

Nevertheless, some commentators believe that any benefits derived from the British possession of nuclear weapons were purchased at a considerable price. They claim that these weapons fostered illusions of grandeur and great-power notions which obscured the reality of Britain's standing in the post-war world. As a consequence of her preoccupation with a world role and nuclear partnership, Britain, it is argued, clung too long to the remnants of empire, and discounted the viability of a role in the European Economic Community.[22] Undoubtedly, President de Gaulle considered that Britain rated her special relationship with Washington above any commitment to Europe, a view confirmed rather than created by the Nassau Agreement.[23] These criticisms, though pertinent, should be qualified. Just as any diplomatic successes of the fifties and early sixties cannot be solely attributed to nuclear weapons (these were only instruments or entry cards which had to be shrewdly used), failures of policy cannot be blamed upon them exclusively. British reluctance to join the EEC was a profoundly complex phenomenon. It cannot simply be explained as a 'continental–oceanic dichotomy'; the whole idea, as one authority has written, 'seemed to go against many time-hallowed traditions of British foreign policy'.[24] While Britain's nuclear aspirations derived from, and contributed to, her great-power notions, they were only one factor amongst several others.

More valid than the criticism about illusions of grandeur is the claim that political dividends from the deterrent have sharply diminished in recent years. Several reasons account for this change. From the mid 1960s onwards, Britain could no longer conceal her decline as a world power, as evidenced by her recurring economic difficulties, her withdrawal from east of Suez, and her abortive attempts to enter the EEC. The nuclear club did not remain exclusive. While there were only three nuclear powers, Britain could bracket herself with the superpowers. Once France and China attained nuclear status, and others gained the technological capacity to follow suit, the superpowers had to take account of these forces, or potential forces. Even more significantly, Britain's nuclear force was dwarfed by the rapid expansion of the Soviet and American strategic arsenals. When Britain purchased her option of sixty-four Polaris launchers at Nassau in 1962, the United States had 1038 launchers and the Soviet Union about 265. Fifteen years later, the United States could deliver 11,330 warheads, the

Soviet Union 3826, and Britain only 192 (but none of the British warheads were separately targeted).[25] From this relative decline in strategic power has come a loss of status and influence. Britain has never been involved in the Strategic Arms Limitation Talks, which have had a bearing not only upon the global balance of power but also upon the security of western Europe. Like other NATO countries, Britain is simply briefed upon the course and conduct of the negotiations. Britain may still derive dividends from her nuclear power, particularly within the confines of NATO, but these dividends are much less extensive than they formerly were.

Unlike the political utility of an independent deterrent, its strategic implications were but slowly realised. The strategy of an independent British nuclear deterrent was not conceived until the early 1950s. The causal factors were twofold: the salutary experience of rearmament during the Korean War which had imposed immense strains upon the economy and the balance of payments, and the sheer size of the conventional force goals of ninety-six divisions set by NATO at the Lisbon meeting of February 1952. Fearing that the British economy could not maintain her allocation of 300,000 troops in Europe, Churchill directed the Chiefs of Staff to undertake a 'new assessment' of British strategy. Their report, known as the 'Global Strategy Paper' of 1952, had a profound effect upon British, American and NATO strategy. Working upon the premise that atomic weapons had revolutionised the nature of war, the joint Chiefs of Staff asserted that any Soviet aggression could be most effectively deterred by the threat of instantaneous atomic attack. They also believed that the threat of using tactical nuclear weapons would enable NATO to reduce her conventional forces and yet still deter the Soviet Union. This paper influenced the 'New Look' of the Eisenhower Administration, the adoption of massive retaliation as an American strategic doctrine, and the revision downwards of NATO force goals in December 1954.[26]

Britain was the first country to base her national defence upon a declared policy of nuclear deterrence. Remnants of this policy still remain inasmuch as Britain secured, under the Nassau Agreement, the right to use her deterrent independently where 'supreme national interests are at stake'.[27] In this role, the deterrent has been justified as a trigger which might unleash far larger American strategic forces or, in the case of American defection, as a weapon of last resort to avert a Soviet attack upon Britain. Both scenarios have been criticised for their lack of credibility and realism. While there is every reason to believe, despite sincere protestations to the contrary, that an American President would be reluctant to risk the destruction of the United States for the sake of western Europe, it seems inherently improbable that he would ever feel forced to do so by an independent British initiative. Similarly, a direct Soviet attack upon Britain is the least likely of the many tortuous scenarios which can be imagined. Should any crisis develop, without the prospect of American intervention, Moscow could simply wait while forcing London or Paris to make the choice between suicide or surrender. As a trigger or as a weapon of last resort, the British deterrent lacks some credibility. Nevertheless, there may still be a valid distinction between actual and perceived credibility.[28] Whatever the actual substance of the British strategic threat, it compounds the uncertainty in Soviet calculations and adds marginally to her defensive problems. The British Polaris fleet may seem puny when compared to the forces of Russia and the United States,[29] but it threatens to destroy major industrial and population centres in the Soviet Union, inflicting some fifteen million to twenty million casualties (virtually the same number that perished during the Great Patriotic War). It would hardly console those people to know that they had been the victims of a puny and relatively insignificant deterrent.

The British nuclear force has also been described as a contribution to the allied deterrent. The contributory theme has been a recurrent feature in the Defence White Papers, usually couched in suitably brief and opaque terminology – the modest contribution of 1957 had become an 'important' contribution by 1960.[30] Various writers have suspected that this vagueness has been other than coincidental. 'Precision', writes Snyder, 'would have revealed the policy's weakness as strategic doctrine and thereby undermined its prestige and symbolic applications.'[31] This is probably true. Britain's nuclear force is committed to the alliance (unlike the French nuclear forces), and its centre of decision is independent of the

American command. Conceivably, its presence could complicate Soviet calculations about the value of using, or of threatening to use, nuclear weapons in the European theatre. But the likelihood of Britain's Polaris fleet acting independently in defence of NATO is extremely remote. A joint allied response would be more likely, in which Britain's four submarines would represent a tiny (and shrinking) proportion of the overall force. Were Britain's deterrent merely intended to contribute to the western deterrent, then its renewal could hardly be justified. It remains basically a national deterrent of 'last resort', a minor complicating factor in Soviet calculations.

Minimum deterrence cannot be verified. It cannot be proved that the possession of a small nuclear force will preserve Britain from a nuclear attack, or from political pressure based upon the threat of such an attack. The credibility of the British deterrent remains a matter of speculation, but any assessment must recognise the technical viability of Polaris as a weapons system. Operating from the continental shelf, the submarines are extremely difficult to detect. The often forecast breakthrough in anti-submarine warfare (ASW) has yet to materialise. As Cyrus Vance, when Secretary of State under President Carter, confirmed, American intelligence neither credits the Soviet Union with an effective ASW capability at the moment, nor with the likelihood of developing such a capability.[32] Furthermore, Polaris A-3 missiles are still likely to penetrate Soviet defences. The Anti-Ballistic Missile (ABM) Treaty of the SALT-1 agreement (1972) has restricted Soviet defences. Only one ABM system of 100 launchers is permitted to guard Moscow, while the rest of the Soviet Union is left undefended. Even Moscow remains vulnerable to British warheads, according to the estimates of the International Institute of Strategic Studies.[33]

Polaris operates within a radically altered strategic context. Globally, the transformation since the early sixties could hardly have been more complete. The 5 : 1 advantage in missile launchers enjoyed by the United States at the time of the Cuban missile crisis has utterly evaporated. From the acute inferiority of seventeen years ago, the strategic rocket forces of the Soviet Union have attained a numerical parity in launchers and some useful advantages in other respects, especially in 'throw weight' (the total weight which a missile can deliver). Within the European theatre, too, significant changes have taken place. While the United States has dismantled its medium-range missiles and reduced the number of its medium-range bombers, the Soviet Union has retained its 600 medium- and intermediate-range ballistic missiles as well as a medium-range bomber force which exceeds its NATO equivalent by 2 : 1. The Soviet Union is now enlarging and modernising these forces by deploying new generations of strike aircraft, the long range Backfire bomber, and the formidable SS-20 missile with its multiple warheads.[34] Massive changes, in short, have occurred in the global and European theatres. The era of American nuclear dominance has ended. The future of the British nuclear deterrent must be considered in light of these circumstances.

Several options are open to the British government. By heeding the advice of some pundits, it could disarm unilaterally, rely upon the residual nuclear cover of the United States, and reap the benefits of leaving the nuclear club. The advantages would seem to be threefold. In the first place, nuclear disarmament would save Britain money; it would save the maintenance and operational costs of Polaris over the next ten to twelve years, which have been estimated at £1500 millions at 1976 prices.[35] Refraining from the deployment of a new ballistic missile force would save between £4000 millions and £5000 millions at 1980 prices over the same period of time. Secondly, nuclear disarmament would enable Britain to avoid several difficult choices in her allocation of funds within the defence vote. Unless the total defence budget was expanded by a substantial amount, in real terms, in the 1980s, the cost of procuring a new nuclear deterrent would have to be balanced by reductions in conventional military expenditure. Conversely, without the expense of another nuclear deterrent, Britain might be able, at least marginally, to enhance her conventional forces. Thirdly, unilateral nuclear disarmament has been advocated as a means by which Britain could take the lead in honouring her commitments under Article VI of the Non-Proliferation Treaty (NPT). By the terms of this Article, Britain is required to pursue 'negotiations in good faith on effective measures relating to the cessation of the nuclear arms race at an early date'. By abandoning the deterrent, it is argued, 'Britain could yet influence the disturbing number of nations which are crowding behind us in the [arms] race'.[36]

Of these arguments, the non-proliferation belief is probably the least substantial. Neither France nor China seems likely to be impressed by an act of self-denial by Britain. Most of the other countries who have not signed the NPT are located in Asia and in the Middle East. As their nuclear pretensions reflect concerns about regional security and prestige, they are unlikely to be much impressed by a British initiative. Those who believe that Britain can influence other states in non-proliferation seem to be suffering from a mirror image of those illusions of grandeur about the role or impact of Britain in world affairs.

To concentrate upon conventional forces has obvious attractions. Each branch of the armed services could benefit from new items of conventional equipment, so enhancing the defence of the United Kingdom base and the capability of British forces in Europe. But problems beset any notion of conventional deterrence. Improved air and sea defences could reduce but not remove the vulnerability of Britain, especially to attacks from bombers or air-to-surface missiles. Britain, as NATO's main reserve base, would remain a prime target should conflict erupt in northern or central Europe. Deterring such conflict by conventional means, that is by maintaining an ability to deny an enemy his military objectives, would impose a considerable, and possibly unacceptable, burden upon the economies of Britain and her European allies. Unless there is a sustained period of economic growth in the 1980s, a long-term improvement in conventional capabilities seems unlikely.[37] Even if these forces are improved radically, they could not deter all forms of conflict; they could not prevent an escalation to limited nuclear or to all-out nuclear war. Ultimately, deterrence requires the threat of nuclear retaliation to complicate Soviet calculations and to augment her uncertainties.[38]

British nuclear disarmament would involve complete reliance upon the strategic nuclear protection of the United States. American commitments are sincerely and repeatedly made. The United States has supported them by the emplacement of 300,000 troops and 7000 tactical nuclear weapons in Europe. She also has massive investments, cultural links and historical ties with many of the countries in western Europe. Although her front-line forces are deployed in the least vulnerable sector of the Central Front, they would almost certainly be involved in any large-scale conventional war. Yet the decision to move beyond the nuclear threshold remains formidably difficult; indeed it would seem reasonable to suppose that an American President would prefer almost any other option. Though no longer self-sufficient, the United States could survive without western Europe. Whether she would survive nuclear release is a very different question. Legitimate doubts remain about the American nuclear commitment.

Saving money is the most convincing reason for abandoning the nuclear deterrent. The savings are hardly huge (about two-and-a-half per cent of the present defence budget, rising to a maximum of ten per cent in the late eighties), but they are real and tangible. Should Britain take this course and remain in NATO, she would have to balance these economic savings against the loss of some political leverage and strategic independence. Arguably the status of Britain as a nuclear power has proved useful within NATO. It can only have assisted Mr Healey in persuading his colleagues to revise NATO's nuclear strategy in 1967. In inter-state bargaining, as Coral Bell has argued, 'the aura of military power may be more important than that power itself'.[39] The Labour government of 1974–9 kept its options open, spending £1000 million on a Polaris Improvement Programme and deciding to make its own tritium for use in warheads rather than to rely on American sources.[40]

Should the government resolve to keep the nuclear deterrent, several options are possible. One option, which is periodically revived, would be some form of Anglo-French nuclear co-operation. Mr Heath endorsed this idea in 1967. In the Godkin Lectures, he suggested the formation of a 'nuclear force based on the existing British and French forces which would be held in trusteeship for Europe as a whole'.[41] Theoretically, the idea had some attractions. If implemented, it could have provided a more viable supplement to the American nuclear guarantee of western Europe. It might also have produced some economic and technological benefits. Access to British knowledge could have diminished the cost of the research, development and manufacture of warheads for France, while access to French industrial capacity might have cut the cost of missile production for Britain.[42]

Political difficulties, however, removed any possibility of co-operation in the late sixties and early seventies. Gaullist governments insisted upon the pure undiluted control of the *force de frappe*. They neither wished to integrate it into NATO nor to Europeanise the objectives of the force, as Mr Heath had suggested. Britain, too, could only have entered an Anglo-French accord at the risk of severing some of her ties with the United States. Hitherto she has received classified information from the United States on the precise condition that she did not reveal it to any other party without American agreement. As Ian Smart concluded, Anglo-French nuclear co-operation was unlikely unless Britain entered 'the partnership alone – without the United States, without NATO and even without the other prospective members of a united Western Europe'.[43] These political obstacles proved insurmountable. Some may have eased with the recent improvement in Franco-American relations. Giscard d'Estaing has modified aspects of Gaullist defence policy, although he still remains wedded to the *force de dissuasion* (having recently authorised production of a sixth submarine). Moreover, the British and French governments will have to review the strategies of their respective deterrents during the course of any SALT-3 negotiations, which are likely to focus, at least partially, on the European theatre. A Franco-British rapprochement is possible; indeed it has already been mooted in the French press.[44] Yet such co-operation is likely to be limited, perhaps confined to targeting and deployment. Unless NATO collapsed, or the Americans withdrew their commitment to Europe's defence, fully-fledged co-operation seems extremely remote. Anglo-French co-operation may be possible in the future, but it can hardly serve as basis for any immediate decision about the renewal of the British deterrent.

As an alternative, the British government could consider the deployment of cruise missiles. Derived from the technology which produced the German V-1 'buzz bomb', the cruise missile is a slow, low-flying robot aircraft which is guided all the way to its target. Advances in small efficient fan-jet engines, airframe materials, miniaturised warheads, and terrain contour matching computers, have transformed this weapons system.

The on-board computers are expected to be able to guide the cruise missile over 2500 miles in flight to within thirty metres of its target. The deployment of such missiles by Britain has been strongly advocated. The cruise missile, some commentators claim, could enhance the deterrent capability of a medium-sized power. They believe that the weapon system would prove to be a relatively cheap option, which could be deployed in both conventional and nuclear modes. By blurring the distinction between nuclear thresholds and conventional intervention, the cruise missile could portend the demise of superpower deterrence. The cruise missile, in short, was considered likely to 'produce a new pattern of international relationships, a more subtle and confused one in which lesser powers have greater influence'.[45]

Some qualifications should be heeded before accepting this argument. Unless deployed aboard existing aircraft, the cruise missile is unlikely to prove a substantially cheaper deterrent. As aircraft would be vulnerable to attacks on their bases and to interception from the formidable Soviet air defences, a sea-launched system remains a more likely option for Britain. It would not be cheap, however. The cost of one cruise missile (between $500,000 and $2,000,000) cannot be compared directly with the cost of one Polaris missile (about $7,000,000).[46] Each Polaris missile carries three MRVed warheads which could strike at three targets in a cluster. To cover the ninety-six targets at the mercy of two Polaris submarines would require at least double the number of cruise-missile-carrying submarines (on the assumption that each boat carried twenty-eight cruise missiles). Allowance would also have to be made for the vulnerability of the slow, low-flying cruise missiles. Some could be detected by airborne 'look down' radar, such as the Soviet MOSS sysem, and shot down either by high-performance interceptors or by the SA-10 surface to air defence missile. Were the penetration efficiency assumed to be eighty per cent (above current American estimates), eleven boats would be needed to match the cover of five Polaris submarines. The development costs would be as expensive as those required to deploy a new ballistic missile force; the annual operating costs would be substantially higher.[47]

Mrs Thatcher's government is more likely to favour a new

submarine-launched ballistic missile (SLBM) force. This deterrent would presumably number five boats, so ensuring that two were always on station. They would carry either new Polaris or Trident I missiles, if the Americans were prepared to sell the latter. The missiles would be armed with multiple warheads (MRVs) and advanced penetration aids. Grasping this nettle, though laudably resolute, would not in itself ensure an 'effective' deterrent into the 1990s and beyond. In the Soviet Union and the United States, advanced research is now under way on the new weapon concepts which could revolutionise nuclear warfare. Scientists in both countries have recognised the potential of charged-particle-beam weaponry in both an anti-satellite and an anti-ballistic missile role. Charged-particle-beam weaponry involves the conversion of colossal amounts of energy into sub-atomic particles which, if shot through the atmosphere in the form of a beam, could disembowel their target. This process requires sophisticated long-range radars able to detect and track re-entry vehicles outside the atmosphere; the ability to generate the beam, to point, track and propagate it through the atmosphere; and the ability to measure any misses, to correct the aim of the beam, and to ensure pin-point accuracy at ranges of 1000 kilometers. Major-General Keegan, formerly of the US Air Force, has suggested that the Soviet Union could be close to deploying an effective charged-particle-beam ABM system in the 1980s.[48]

Although the Carter Administration initially discounted the views of Major-General Keegan, it has subsequently launched a heavy investment into charged-particle-beam research.[49] Whatever the outcome of this research and any pertinent arms control negotiations, a British government, wedded to the retention of an independent deterrent, must watch developments closely. The British deterrent, by refinements of its re-entry vehicle, could still overcome an ABM system based upon charged-particle-beams. By ejecting decoys or chaff, the re-entry vehicle could confuse long-range radar and deflect the fine pointing of a beam. By exploding nuclear devices outside the atmosphere, it could disturb the earth's magnetic field, bend the beam, and help to ensure the survival of the re-entry vehicle. At the moment, all technological options are not foreclosed.[50] But it should be stressed that renewing the deterrent represents a continuing commitment to keep abreast of developments in nuclear weaponry, within the limits of Britain's economic and technological capacity.

It seems likely that Britain will remain a nuclear power, in spite of the massive changes which have occurred, both nationally and internationally, since 1947. The nuclear deterrent is no longer a guarantee of great-power status; it is not an invitation card to superpower diplomacy. The political utility of the British nuclear deterrent has declined sharply. The only remaining dividends are the technical and scientific links with the United States, the participation in various arms control negotiations, and some leverage within NATO. Paradoxically, the strategic arguments in favour of an independent nuclear deterrent seem to have increased in recent years. The shift of strategic power, both globally and within the European theatre, underlines the advantages of retaining an independent weapon of last resort, a complicating factor in Soviet calculations. Given its current feasibility as an economic and technological proposition, the nuclear deterrent is not an option which should be too readily aborted.

Notes and References

Crown copyright material is reproduced with kind permission of Her Majesty's Stationery Office.

INTRODUCTION   *David Dilks*

1. CAB. 37/160/20: memorandum by Lord Grey (27 Nov 1916).
2. M. E. Howard, *The Mediterranean Strategy in the Second World War* (Weidenfeld and Nicolson, 1968), pp. 7–8.
3. E. L. Woodward, *British Foreign Policy in the Second World War*, (HMSO, 1970) vol. I, p. xliv.
4. D. N. Dilks (ed.), *The Diaries of Sir Alexander Cadogan* (Cassell, 1971) p. 321.
5. R. L. Tree, *When the Moon was High* (Macmillan, 1975) p. 144.
6. *Hansard*, 5th ser., HC, CCCLXII, 54.
7. Earl of Halifax, *Fulness of Days* (Collins, 1957) p. 257.
8. R. E. Sherwood, *The White House Papers of Harry L. Hopkins* (Eyre and Spottiswoode, 1949) vol. II, pp. 714, 717.
9. WP(42)48, CAB. 66/21: memorandum by A. Eden (28 Jan 1942).
10. F.O. 954/26: A. Eden to W. S. Churchill (16 Mar 1943).
11. Lord Avon, *The Eden Memoirs: The Reckoning* (Cassell, 1965) p. 545.
12. D. N. Dilks (ed.), *The Diaries of Sir Alexander Cadogan* (Cassell, 1971) p. 537.
13. WP(42)516, CAB. 66/30: memorandum by A. Eden (8 Nov 1942).
14. F.O. 954/26: W. S. Churchill to Sir A. Clark Kerr (16 June 1943).
15. Lord Avon, *The Eden Memoirs: The Reckoning* (Cassell, 1965) p. 439.
16. PREM. 3/355/13: W. S. Churchill to Attlee and War Cabinet (17 Oct 1944).
17. Lord Avon, *The Eden Memoirs: The Reckoning* (Cassell, 1965) p. 525.
18. WP(44)414, PRO CAB. 66/53: memorandum by C. R. Attlee (26 July 1944).
19. W. G. Hayter, *The Kremlin and the Embassy* (Hodder and Stoughton, 1966) p. 28; *The Memoirs of General the Lord Ismay* (Heinemann, 1960) p. 403.
20. Earl of Birkenhead, *Halifax* (Hamish Hamilton, 1965) p. 537.
21. W. K. Hancock and M. M. Gowing, *British War Economy* (HMSO, 1949) pp. 546–9.
22. R. F. Harrod, *The Life of John Maynard Keynes* (Macmillan, 1952) p. 596.
23. H. Dalton, *The Fateful Years* (Muller, 1957) pp. 77–8.
24. D. LePan, *Bright Glass of Memory* (Toronto: McGraw-Hill Ryerson, 1979) pp. 86–7, 104.
25. Dalton's diary, vol. 33 (19 Dec 1945). I am indebted to the British Library of Political and Economic Science, LSE, for permission to reprint material from the Dalton Papers.
26. Ibid., vol. 33 (7 Dec 1945).
27. Ibid., vol. 33 (5 Oct 1945).
28. CAB. 128/7: Cab[inet]. con[clusions]. (1 Jan 1946), confidential annexe.
29. Dalton's diary, vol. 33 (7 Dec 1945).
30. Ibid., vol. 33 (17 Oct 1945).
31. Ibid., vol. 34 (9 Feb 1946).

32. CAB. 129/1: memorandum by C. R. Attlee (1 Sep 1945).
33. Dalton's diary, vol. 34 (18 Feb 1946).
34. Ibid., vol. 34 (29 Mar 1946).
35. Lord Strang, *Home and Abroad* (Deutsch, 1956) p. 287.
36. Dalton's diary, vol. 34 (9 Sep 1946).
37. D. N. Dilks (ed.), *The Diaries of Sir Alexander Cadogan* (Cassell, 1971) p. 189.
38. A. J. Toynbee, *Experiences* (Oxford University Press, 1969) p. 52.
39. Dalton's diary, vol. 34 (9 Sep 1946).
40. Ibid., vol. 34 (5 Oct 1946).
41. Dalton papers 9/2, British Library of Political and Economic Science, LSE: H. Dalton to C. R. Attlee (28 Nov 1946); cf. H. Dalton to J. Snyder (25 Nov 1946).
42. Lord Strang, *Home and Abroad* (Deutsch, 1956) p. 291.
43. *The Memoirs of Field-Marshal Montgomery* (Collins, 1960 edition) p. 444.
44. Dalton papers 9/3, British Library of Political and Economic Science, LSE: H. Dalton to C. R. Attlee (20 Jan 1947), and enclosure.
45. Ibid.; Dalton's diary, vol. 35 (27 Jan 1947).
46. CAB. 129/19: memorandum by E. Bevin (5 July 1947).
47. Nigel Nicolson (ed.), *Harold Nicolson: Diaries and Letters 1945–1962* (Collins, 1968) pp. 115–16.
48. CAB. 129/24: memorandum by E. Bevin (4 Jan 1948).
49. CAB. 129/25: memorandum by E. Bevin (3 Mar 1948); CAB. 128/12 and 14: Cab. con. (5 Mar 1948) and confidential annexe.
50. Lord Strang, *Home and Abroad* (Deutsch, 1956) pp. 297–8.
51. CAB. 128/13: Cab. con. (26 July 1948).
52. CAB. 128/13: Cab. con. (22 Sep 1948).
53. CAB. 128/15: Cab. con. (17 Jan 1949).
54. CAB. 129/36 (2): memorandum by E. Bevin (25 Aug 1949).
55. CAB. 128/13: Cab. con. (13 Dec 1948); CAB. 128/15: Cab. con. (8 Mar, 5 and 9 May 1949).
56. CAB. 128/15 and 16: Cab. con. (26 May, 29 Aug, 15 Dec 1949).
57. The late Mr Creech-Jones recounted this to the author in 1960.
58. *Hansard*, 5th ser., HC, DLXI, 36–8.
59. I. Kirkpatrick, *The Inner Circle* (Macmillan, 1959) p. 261.
60. Ibid., p. 262; Lord Avon, *The Eden Memoirs: Full Circle* (Cassell, 1960) p. 358.

1. THE TWILIGHT WAR AND THE FALL OF FRANCE: CHAMBERLAIN AND CHURCHILL
IN 1940 *David Dilks*

1. Neville Chamberlain to Hilda Chamberlain (15 July 1939). These letters, and Chamberlain's diaries, are held by the University of Birmingham, to which I am obliged for permission to print extracts.
2. Neville Chamberlain to Ida Chamberlain (5 Aug 1939).
3. Neville Chamberlain to Ida Chamberlain (8 Oct 1939).
4. W. S. Churchill. *The Second World War*, vol. 1 (Cassell, 1948) pp. 373–4, hereinafter cited as *S.W.W.*
5. Neville Chamberlain to Hilda Chamberlain (26 Nov 1939).
6. N.C. 7/9/49: Churchill to Chamberlain (15 Sep 1939). This correspondence is preserved in the Chamberlain papers.
7. N.C. 7/9/50: Chamberlain to Churchill (16 Sep 1939).
8. N.C. 7/9/51: Churchill to Chamberlain (18 Sep 1939).
9. N.C. 7/9/53: Churchill to Chamberlain (22 Sep 1939); Neville Chamberlain to Ida Chamberlain (23 Sep 1939).

10. Neville Chamberlain to Hilda Chamberlain (17 Sep 1939).

11. N.C. 7/9/63: memorandum by Sir Horace Wilson (3 Oct 1939); Neville Chamberlain to Ida Chamberlain (8 Oct 1939).

12. *The War Speeches of the Rt Hon. Winston S. Churchill* (Cassell, 1952) vol. I, p. 119.

13. F.O. 800/328: Churchill to Halifax (15 Jan 1940).

14. *War Speeches of the Rt Hon. Winston S. Churchill*, vol. I, p. 137; *S.W.W.*, vol. I, p. 488.

15. Neville Chamberlain to Ida Chamberlain (27 Jan 1940).

16. W.M.(55)40, CAB. 65/5; Neville Chamberlain to Ida Chamberlain (16 Mar 1940).

17. Neville Chamberlain to Ida Chamberlain (16 Mar 1940).

18. F.O. 800/328: Churchill to Halifax (14 Mar 1940).

19. *War Speeches of the Rt Hon. Winston S. Churchill*, vol. I, p. 155; *S.W.W.* vol. I, pp. 526–7.

20. Neville Chamberlain to Hilda Chamberlain (10 Mar 1940), and to Ida Chamberlain (30 Mar 1940).

21. Neville Chamberlain to Ida Chamberlain (13 Apr 1940).

22. Neville Chamberlain to Hilda Chamberlain (20 Apr 1940).

23. Neville Chamberlain to Ida Chamberlain (27 Apr 1940).

24. Neville Chamberlain to Hilda Chamberlain (4 May 1940).

25. *S.W.W.* vol. I, p. 595.

26. K. G. Feiling, *The Life of Neville Chamberlain* (Macmillan, 1946) p. 442.

27. Neville Chamberlain to Hilda Chamberlain (17 May 1940).

28. D. N. Dilks (ed.), *The Diaries of Sir Alexander Cadogan* (Cassell, 1971) p. 284; *S.W.W.* vol. II, p. 48; S. S. Wilson, *The Cabinet Office to 1945* (HMSO, 1975) p. 104.

29. Chamberlain's diary (21 and 26 May 1940).

30. Ibid. (28 May 1940).

31. G/4/5/48, Lloyd George papers (now in the Library of the House of Lords): Churchill to Lloyd George (29 May 1940).

32. Chamberlain's diary (5 June 1940).

33. *War Speeches of the Rt Hon. Winston S. Churchill*, vol. I, p. 199.

34. Chamberlain's diary (18 June 1940), and his letter to Ida Chamberlain (21 June 1940).

35. F. Lloyd George, *The Years that are Past* (Hutchinson, 1967) p. 264; Neville Chamberlain to Ida Chamberlain (21 June 1940).

36. N.C. 7/9/89: Churchill to Chamberlain (1 July 1940).

37. Chamberlain's diary (9 Sep 1940).

38. R. Rhodes James, *Victor Cazalet* (Hamish Hamilton, 1976) p. 278.

2. WAR AND FOREIGN POLICY: 1939–45   *The late Lord Strang*

1. *S.W.W.* vol. IV, p. 234.

2. E. L. Woodward, *British Foreign Policy in the Second World War* (HMSO, 1962) p. xxx.

3. C. de Gaulle, *The Call to Honour* (Weidenfeld and Nicolson, 1955) pp. 167–8; Lord Templewood (formerly Sir Samuel Hoare), *Ambassador on Special Mission* (Collins, 1946) passim.

4. W. H. McNeill, *America, Britain and Russia* (Oxford University Press, 1953) p. 17.

5. Earl of Birkenhead, *Halifax* (Hamish Hamilton, 1965) p. 496.

6. Lord Avon (formerly Sir Anthony Eden), *The Eden Memoirs: The Reckoning* (Cassell, 1965) p. 286; *S.W.W.* vol. III, p. 539.

7. *S.W.W.* vol. III, p. 21.

8. *S.W.W.* vol. II, pp. 494–501.

9. C. Hull, *The Memoirs of Cordell Hull* (Hodder and Stoughton, 1948) vol. II, p. 1333.
10. W. L. Langer, *Our Vichy Gamble* (New York: W. W. Norton and Co., 1947) p. 266.
11. Lord Avon, *The Eden Memoirs: The Reckoning*, p. 361.
12. Ibid., p. 447.
13. R. E. Sherwood, *The White House Papers of Harry L. Hopkins*, 2 vols (Eyre and Spottiswoode, 1948, 1949) vol. II, p. 849.
14. M. Matloff and E. M. Snell, *Strategic Planning for Coalition Warfare* (Department of the Army, Washington, 1953) pp. 29–30.
15. Lord Avon, *The Eden Memoirs: The Reckoning*, pp. 144, 146, 176; E. L. Woodward, 'Some Reflections on British Policy, 1939–45', *International Affairs*, XXXI (1955) 280.
16. *S.W.W.* vol. I, p. 601.
17. Lord Avon, *The Eden Memoirs: The Reckoning*, p. 404
18. F. L. Loewenheim, H. D. Langley and M. Jonas, *Roosevelt and Churchill: their secret wartime correspondence* (New York: Saturday Review Press, 1975).
19. For examples, see K. R. Greenfield, *American Strategy in World War II* (Baltimore: Johns Hopkins Press, 1963).
20. A. Bryant, *The Turn of the Tide* (Collins, 1957) pp. 21–2.
21. Sherwood, *The White House Papers of Harry L. Hopkins*, vol. I, p. 202; vol. II, p. 638.
22. Lord Avon, *The Eden Memoirs: The Reckoning* (Cassell, 1965) p. 374.
23. W. H. McNeill, *America, Britain and Russia* (Oxford University Press, 1953) p. 461n.
24. *S.W.W.* vol. VI, p. 234.
25. Sherwood, *The White House Papers of Harry L. Hopkins*, vol. II, p. 726.
26. *S.W.W.* vol. VI, pp. 399, 400.
27. Ibid., p. 297.
28. S. F. Bemis, *A Diplomatic History of the United States* (New York: Henry Holt, 1955) pp. 636–7.
29. K. G. Feiling, *The Life of Neville Chamberlain* (Macmillan, 1946) p. 367; *Hansard*, 5th ser., HC, CCCXXXIX. 49.
30. H. L. Stimson and McG. Bundy, *On Active Service in Peace and War* (New York: Harper and Brothers, 1948) p. 644.
31. *Hansard*, 5th ser., HC, CCCCVIII, 1284.
32. *S.W.W.* vol. VI, pp. 351–2.
33. *Hansard*, 5th ser., HC, CCCCXIII, 291.
34. W. H. McNeill, *America, Britain and Russia* (Oxford University Press, 1953) p. 536.
35. For fuller descriptions of the Commission's work, see Lord Strang, *Home and Abroad* (Deutsch, 1956) pp. 199–225; and E. L. Woodward, *British Foreign Policy in the Second World War* (HMSO, 1971, 1976) vols II, III, V.
36. Sherwood, *The White House Papers of Harry L. Hopkins*, vol. II, p. 712.
37. J. E. Smith, *The Defence of Berlin* (Johns Hopkins and Oxford University Press, 1963).
38. Lord Avon, *The Eden Memoirs: The Reckoning* Foreword.
39. *The Memoirs of General the Lord Ismay* (Heinemann, 1960) p. 199.
40. R. E. Sherwood, *The White House Papers of Harry L. Hopkins*, 2 vols (Eyre and Spottiswoode, 1948, 1949) vol. II, p. 644.

Since Lord Strang wrote this essay, many sources of information about British foreign policy during the war have become available. A number of them are referred to in the notes above. The most comprehensive account is that given by E. L. Woodward, *British foreign policy in the Second World War* (HMSO, 1-volume edition, 1962; 5-volume edition 1970–6). Other important material may be found in C. Thorne, *Allies of a Kind* (Hamish

Hamilton, 1978); J. Harvey (ed.), *The War Diaries of Oliver Harvey* (Collins, 1978); P. Lowe, *Great Britain and the origins of the Pacific War* (Clarendon Press, 1977); D. N. Dilks (ed.), *The Diaries of Sir Alexander Cadogan* (Cassell, 1971); *The Memoirs of Lord Gladwyn* (Weidenfeld and Nicolson, 1972); R. Dallek, *Franklin D. Roosevelt and American Foreign Policy, 1932–1945* (New York: Oxford University Press, 1979); J. M. Burns, *Roosevelt, the Soldier of Freedom* (New York: Harcourt Brace, 1970); E. Barker, *Churchill and Eden at War* (Macmillan, 1978); *Foreign Relations of the United States* (Department of State, Washington) normally 5 vols p.a., supplemented by separate collections of documents on *The Conferences at Cairo and Teheran, The Conferences at Malta and Yalta, The Conference at Potsdam* (Washington, 1961, 1955, 1960); *Correspondence between the Chairman of the Council of Ministers and the Presidents of the U.S.A. and the Prime Ministers of Great Britain, 1941–5* (Moscow, 1957).

The voluminous papers now available for research in the Public Record Office, London, include the War Cabinet's conclusions, CAB. 65/1–54; its memoranda, CAB. 66/1–67; the Private Office papers of Mr Anthony Eden, 1940–5, F.O. 954/1–34; Private Office papers of Lord Halifax, F.O. 800/309–28; general political correspondence of the Foreign Office in F.O. 371.

3. OPERATION BRACELET: CHURCHILL IN MOSCOW, 1942   *Graham Ross*

1. See Moran; Churchill's account appears in *S.W.W.* vol. IV.

2. Sir John Wheeler-Bennett (ed.), *Action this Day* (Macmillan, 1969). See especially pp. 250–5.

3. The main Public Record Office files concerning Bracelet are: PREM. 3, 76/1 to 12; PREM. 3, 392/1 and 2; PREM. 4, 71/4; F.O. 800/300 and F.O. 800/402; Clark Kerr's account is in F.O. 800/300, pp. 117–48 and Cadogan's letter to Eden is in F.O. 800/402. The same file also contains a complete set of the British records of the conference. Other sets, for example WP(42)373 in CAB. 66/28, do not include the record of Churchill's final meeting with Stalin. All these documents are Crown Copyright and are quoted by permission of the Controller, Her Majesty's Stationery Office.

4. And see Nigel Nicolson (ed.), *Harold Nicolson: Diaries and Letters 1939–45* (Collins, 1967) entries for 14 Jan and 22 June 1942.

5. Ibid.

6. CAB. 65/27, WM(42)96.

7. On the lack of discussion about strategy see A. J. P. Taylor, *Beaverbrook* (Hamish Hamilton, 1972) p. 488, and *The Memoirs of General the Lord Ismay* (Heinemann, 1960) p. 231. On the mission in general, see CAB. 66/19, WP(41)238.

8. On Eden's visit to Moscow, see PREM. 3, 394/1 to 4. On the treaty see CAB. 66/24, WP(42)220. On possible difficulties in Britain see PREM. 3, 399/8. On American views, see *F.R.U.S.* (1942) vol. III, pp. 494–564, passim.

9. F.O. 371/37028: minute by G. M. Wilson (5 Sep 1943) on how to handle the question of Soviet frontiers at the forthcoming Moscow conference of Foreign Ministers.

10. CAB. 65/30 WM(42)68: (26 May 1942).

11. PREM. 4, 27/9.

12. F.O. 371/32905: minute by Sir Orme Sargent (5 Feb 1942) on the possible course of the Russo-German war.

13. See various references to this in F.O. 371/32906–32908. These rumours were picked up from Stockholm, Ankara, the Vatican and the Free French, between March and June.

14. F.O. 371/32863: paper by Christopher Warner (11 Mar 1942), telegram from Foreign Office to Washington (15 Apr 1942).

15. F.O. 371/32910: minutes by Sargent and Cadogan (both dated 22 July 1942) on a report from Stockholm about alleged German peace feelers towards Russia.

16. On Molotov's priorities see *F.R.U.S.* vol. III, p. 559: Winant to Hull (24 May 1942). For Foreign Office dislike of the Washington communiqué, see F.O. 271/32909: minutes by Cadogan and Eden (30 June 1942).

17. CAB. 66/19, WP(41)272: correspondence between Eden and Cripps. On Cripps's recall, see CAB. 65/29, WM(42)1. On Clark Kerr's appointment, see F.O. 800/300/, p. 128: conversation between Clark Kerr and Cadogan.

18. T. Barman, *Diplomatic Correspondent* (Hamish Hamilton, 1968) p. 8.

19. PREM. 3, 76/1: telegrams from Clark Kerr to the Foreign Office (28 June and 5 July 1942).

20. *Stalin's Correspondence with Churchill and Attlee 1941–45* (New York: Capricorn Books, 1965) p. 56. Roosevelt's 171 to Churchill. All references to the Roosevelt–Churchill correspondence are on a microfilm made available by the National Archives and Records Service of the letters held at the Roosevelt Library, Hyde Park, New York.

21. For Masaryk's proposal, see PREM. 3, 459, pp. 53–5. For Churchill's subsequent comments, see PREM. 4, 71/4, p. 1216: statement by his principal Private Secretary, J. M. Martin (7 Aug 1942).

22. CAB. 79/22: P.M.'s personal minute D 139/2 to Chiefs of Staff. The reference was to a proposal to send planes to the Caucasus.

23. PREM. 3, 76/1: Clark Kerr to Cadogan (28 July 1942).

24. Ibid.: manuscript note from Cadogan to Eden (29 July 1942).

25. *S.W.W.* vol. IV, p. 409. PREM. 4, 71/4, pp. 1200, 1217–20. These citations are from the report on a suspected security leak dated 11 August. Some care was taken to establish when and to whom Churchill spoke of a trip to Moscow.

26. CAB. 65/27, WM(42)100.

27. Moran, p. 47. But he is clearly wrong in dating this meeting 28 July.

28. CAB. 65/27, WM(42)103: (4 Aug 1942). Cripps says the idea was mooted before Churchill's departure and this seems the most likely occasion. See also E. Abel and W. A. Harriman, *Special Envoy to Churchill and Stalin 1941–46* (Hutchinson, 1976) p. 146.

29. *Stalin's correspondence with Churchill and Attlee 1941–45* (New York: Capricorn Books, 1965) pp. 58–9. F.O. 800/402: Sir R. Campbell (Washington) to the Foreign Office (1 Aug 1942).

30. PREM. 3, 76/3: Eden to Churchill (4 Aug and latter's reply on 5 Aug 1942). E. Abel and W. A. Harriman, *Special Envoy to Churchill and Stalin 1941–46* (Hutchinson, 1976) p. 147. Roosevelt–Churchill correspondence: Churchill's 126A to Roosevelt.

31. Lord Tedder, *With Prejudice* (Cassell, 1966) pp. 328, 338–9. F.O. 800/402: Cadogan to Eden (18 Aug 1942).

32. F.O. 800/300, p. 120. Clark Kerr's account is the only version we have of this conversation with Churchill. For his tactics with the Americans, *cf.* R. Parkinson, *Blood, Toil, Tears and Sweat* (Hart-Davis, 1973) p. 454.

33. F.O. 800/300, p. 123: Clark Kerr's manuscript account. For Cadogan's comments, see F.O. 800/402: minute by P. N. Loxley (29 Aug 1942).

34. PREM. 3, 76/3: Churchill's telegram Reflex 85 (13 Aug 1942); *F.R.U.S*, vol. III, pp. 618–19; Moran, pp. 55–6; F.O. 800/300, p. 123.

35. F.O. 800/300, pp. 124–5.

36. *S.W.W.* vol. IV, p. 436. F.O. 800/402: British records of the conference.

37. Halifax Papers 410/4/16: Cadogan to Halifax (29 Aug 1942). Lord Tedder, *With Prejudice* (Cassell, 1966) p. 330.

38. E. Abel and W. A. Harriman, *Special Envoy to Churchill and Stalin 1941–46* (Hutchinson, 1976) p. 155; *S.W.W.* vol. IV, p. 436.

39. PREM. 3, 76/11: memorandum for meeting with Stalin.

40. *F.R.U.S.* vol. III, p. 622: Harriman to Roosevelt (14 Aug 1942); Halifax Papers

410/4/16: Cadogan to Halifax (29 Aug 1942); PREM: 3, 76/11: Jacob to Hollis, private letter (16 Aug 1942); Sir John Wheeler-Bennett (ed.), *Action this Day* (Macmillan, 1969) p. 215; Lord Tedder, *With Prejudice* (Cassell, 1966) p. 337.

41. Lord Avon, *The Eden Memoirs: The Reckoning* (Casssell, 1965) p. 295; *The Memoirs of General the Lord Ismay* (Heinemann, 1960) p. 230; PREM. 3, 76/11: manuscript note from Harriman to Churchill; E. Abel and W. A. Harriman, *Special Envoy to Churchill and Stalin 1941–46* (Hutchinson, 1976) p. 159; *F.R.U.S.* vol. III, p. 622.

42. F.O. 800/402: Cadogan to Eden (18 Aug 1942); F.O. 800/300, p. 127, for Clark Kerr's row with Churchill; see also Moran, p. 58. For the draft telegram about the dinner, see F.O. 800/300, p. 101, and for the transmitted version, PREM. 3, 76/3: Reflex telegram 93 (14 Aug 1942).

43. PREM. 3, 76/11: Clark Kerr to the Foreign Office (16 Aug 1942).

44. CAB. 65/31 WM(42)112. PREM. 3, 395/18: Cadogan minute (14 Aug 1942), Cadogan to Rowan (15 Aug 1942), undated minute by Clark Kerr.

45. Lord Tedder, *With Prejudice* (Cassell, 1966) pp. 337–8; Moran, pp. 58–61; F.O. 800/402: Cadogan to Eden (18 Aug 1942); PREM. 3, 76/11: Clark Kerr to the Foreign Office (16 Aug 1942); F.O. 800/300: pp. 130–4. On Churchill's dislike of interpreters *cf.* E. Abel and W. A. Harriman, *Special Envoy to Churchill and Stalin 1941–46* (Hutchinson, 1976) p. 157.

46. F.O. 800/300, pp. 135–6 and 151 for Reed's letter written to a colleague at the embassy identified only as 'Jim'. Most of the embassy staff were still in Kuibyshev. *Cf.* Moran, p. 61.

47. F.O. 800/300, pp. 136–45. There is no other record of what the two men said.

48. F.O. 800/402: Cadogan to Eden (18 Aug 1942); Moran, p. 62; Svetlana Alliluyeva, *Letters to a Friend* (Hutchinson, 1967) p. 183.

49. A. H. Birse, *Memoirs of an Interpreter* (Michael Joseph, 1967), pp. 94–7.

50. F.O. 800/402: Cadogan to Eden (18 Aug 1942); Halifax Papers 410/4/16: Cadogan to Halifax (29 Aug 1942); F.O. 800/300, p. 146; A. H. Birse, *Memoirs of an Interpreter* (Michael Joseph, 1967) pp. 103–4; *S.W.W.* vol. IV, p. 446 *et seq*; Moran, pp. 62–3.

51. Churchill made some amendments to Birse's notes. See PREM. 3, 76/12.

52. F.O, 800/300, pp. 147, 152.

53. PREM. 3, 76/10: Clark Kerr to Cadogan (20 Aug 1942); PREM. 3, 76/11: Clark Kerr to Foreign Office (16 Aug 1942); PREM. 4, 73/4: Churchill's off the record comments to correspondents in Cairo (22 Aug 1942); F.O. 371/32912: note (26 Aug 1942) on Benes's report of Soviet reaction; F.O. 371/32913: Clark Kerr to Foreign Office (9 Sep 1942) on views of Norwegian ambassador; F.O. 371/32926: Clark Kerr to Foreign Office (31 Oct 1942) on Standley's reaction.

54. M. Matloff and E. M. Snell, *Strategic Planning for Coalition Warfare 1941–42* (GPO Washington, 1953) p. 310; M. Howard, *Grand Strategy* (HMSO, 1972) vol. IV, p. 34; *Stalin's Correspondence with Churchill and Attlee 1941–45* (New York: Capricorn Books, 1965) p. 72.

55. Roosevelt–Churchill correspondence: Churchill's 140 to Roosevelt, Roosevelt's 191 to Churchill; *Stalin's Correspondence with Churchill and Attlee 1941–45* (New York: Capricorn Books, 1965) p. 65, 71, 73–4.

56. See PREM. 3, 392/3 passim: on the Drummond mission; A. H. Birse, *Memoirs of an Interpreter* (Michael Joseph, 1967) pp. 128–9.

57. F.O. 371/32955: minute by Cadogan (28 Aug 1942); *F.R.U.S.* vol. III, pp. 738–40, 753–4; F.O. 371/36929: revised note by Brigadier Firebrace on the working of the 1942 agreement (4 Sep 1943); F.O. 371/36929: Lyttleton to Eden (23 Aug 1943); F.O. 371/43412: minute by Pott (18 May 1944) summarising the position at that time on the 1942 agreement; F.O. 371/47849: letter from Christopher Warner to Ministry of

Production (29 Apr 1945); F.O. 371/47850: Lyttleton to Churchill (2 June 1945); Churchill to Lyttleton (18 June 1945); and see PREM. 3, 396/14 passim.

4. BRITAIN, AMERICA AND THE BOMB   *Margaret Gowing*

1. N. Bohr and J. A. Wheeler, 'The Mechanism of Nuclear Fission', *Physical Review*, LVI (1939) 426.
2. The covering memorandum is in R. W. Clark, *Tizard* (Methuen, 1965) pp. 215–17. The detailed report is in M. Gowing, *Britain and Atomic Energy 1939–1945* (Macmillan, 1964) app. 1, pp. 389–93.
3. M. Gowing, *Britain and Atomic Energy 1939–1945* (Macmillan, 1964) app. 2, pp. 394–436.
4. Ibid., app. 4, pp. 439–40.
5. Ibid., app. 8, p. 447.
6. M. Gowing, *Independence and Deterrence: Britain and Atomic Energy 1945–1952* (Macmillan, 1974) vol. 1 (*Policy Making*), app. 8, pp. 194–206.
7. Ibid., app. 4, pp. 82–4.
8. Ibid., app. 9, pp. 266–72.
9. Dean Acheson, *Present at the Creation* (Hamish Hamilton, 1970) p. 484 and 'Dean Acheson talks to Kenneth Harris', *The Listener* (8 Apr 1970).

This article is based on Professor Gowing's three volumes of atomic energy history – *Britain and Atomic Energy 1939–1945* and *Independence and Deterrence: Britain and Atomic Energy 1945–1952* (volume 1 *Policy Making* and volume II *Policy Execution*). These were written with access to official records in the United Kingdom Atomic Energy Authority and in government departments. No specific references to such records are included in this article because of the complications. Some papers have been refiled since the books were written; some now have Public Record Office reference numbers (instead of the original departmental references), of which some are now open in the PRO and some are not. Some files are still closed in departments. Detailed lists of the documents and files referred to (with PRO references where known) are available from the Authority Historian's Office, Building 328, AERE Harwell, Didcot, Oxon.

5. NEHRU AND THE COMMONWEALTH   *Sarvepalli Gopal*

1. A. H. Hanson and J. Douglas, *India's Democracy* (Weidenfeld and Nicolson, 1972) p. 219.
2. T. B. Millar (ed.), *Australian Foreign Minister: The Diaries of R. G. Casey* (London: Collins, 1972) p. 115.
3. M. Lipton and J. Firn, *The Erosion of a Relationship: India and Britain since 1960* (Oxford: OUP, 1975).
4. Nehru's report on the Commonwealth Conference, Nehru Papers (7 May 1949).
5. See *F.R.U.S.* vol. III, pp. 177–8: report of Dr Grady, first United States ambassador in Delhi, to State Department (26 Dec 1947).
6. Nehru Papers: Nehru's note (12 Sep 1948).
7. Krishna Menon's telegram to Nehru, Nehru Papers (27 Nov 1948).
8. Nehru to J. Narayan, Nehru Papers (14 May 1949).
9. *National Herald* (14 Apr 1953): speech at Delhi, 13 April.
10. Quoted in H. Tinker, *Separate and Unequal: India and the Indians in the British Commonwealth, 1920–50* (OUP, 1976) p. 388.

11. Churchill to Nehru, Nehru Papers (1 July 1953).
12. Churchill to Nehru, Nehru Papers (21 Feb 1955).
13. I. McDonald, *A Man of the Times* (1976) p. 144.
14. Nehru to Nasser, Nehru Papers (2 Aug 1956).
15. Nehru to Nasser, Nehru Papers (5 Aug 1956).
16. Nehru to Eden, Nehru Papers (14 Sep 1956).
17. Malcolm MacDonald, *Titans and Others* (Collins, 1972) p. 224.
18. Quoted in R. Braddon, *Suez: Splitting of a Nation* (Collins, 1973) p. 195.
19. Harold Macmillan, *Riding the Storm 1956–1959* (Macmillan, 1971) pp. 388–9.
20. 'The Future of the Commonwealth', *The Round Table*, XLVI, no. 183 (June 1956) 219.
21. Malcolm Muggeridge, *The Chronicles of Wasted Time – Part I: The Green Stick* (Morrow, 1972) p. 115.
22. John Kenneth Galbraith, 'Democracy, Leadership, Commitment', *Listener* (31 Mar 1977).

Material from the Nehru Papers is cited by courtesy of Mrs Indira Gandhi.

Further accounts of Nehru's life and thought may be found in:
M. Brecher, *Nehru* (OUP, 1959).
M. Brecher, 'India's Decision to Remain in the Commonwealth', *Journal of Commonwealth and Comparative Politics* (March and July 1974).
P. N. S. Mansergh, *The Commonwealth Experience* (London: Weidenfield and Nicolson, 1969).
J. D. B. Miller, *Survey of Commonwealth Affairs: Problems of Expansion and Attrition 1953–1969* (Oxford: OUP, 1974).
H. Tinker, *Separate and Unequal.*

6. THE BRITISH NUCLEAR DETERRENT: PROBLEMS AND POSSIBILITIES   *Edward Spiers*

1. *The Times* (12 Oct 1977) p. 2.
2. I. Smart, *The Future of the British Deterrent: Technical, Economic and Strategic Issues* (The Royal Institute of International Affairs, 1977) pp. 51–3 and 55–8.
3. H. Macmillan, *At the End of the Day, 1961–1963* (Macmillan, 1973) p. 363.
4. *Twelfth Report of the Expenditure Committee*, Cmnd. 399 (1972–3) XXII, pp. xxii and xv.
5. R. Burt, 'The Scope and Limits of SALT', *Foreign Affairs*, LVI (July 1978) 763.
6. M. M. Gowing, *Britain and Atomic Energy* (Macmillan, 1964) app. 2, p. 395.
7. M. M. Gowing, *Independence and Deterrence: Britain and Atomic Energy 1945–1952*, 2 vols (Macmillan, 1974) vol. I, pp. 182–3.
8. A. J. Pierre, *Nuclear Politics: the British Experience with an Independent Strategic Force, 1939–1970* (Oxford University Press, 1972) p. 74.
9. A Goldberg, 'The Military Origins of the British Nuclear Deterrent', *International Affairs*, XL (1964) 606. See also M. M. Gowing, *Independence and Deterrence: Britain and Atomic Energy 1945–1952* (Macmillan, 1974) vol. I, p. 174.
10. C. J. Bartlett, *The Long Retreat: A Short History of British Defence Policy, 1945–70* (Macmillan, 1972) pp. 12–13.
11. F. Williams, *A Prime Minister Remembers* (Heinemann, 1961) p. 119.
12. A. Goldberg, 'The Atomic Origins of the British Nuclear Deterrent', *International Affairs*, XL (1964) 427.
13. Pierre, *Nuclear Politics*, p. 127.
14. E. Young, *A Farewell to Arms Control* (Penguin, 1972) pp. 41–3.

15. R. Osgood, *NATO: The Entangling Alliance* (University of Chicago Press, 1962) p. 267.

16. *Amendment of Agreement between the Government of the United Kingdom of Great Britain and Northern Ireland and the Government of the United States of America for Co-operation on the Uses of Atomic Energy for Mutual Defence Purposes of July 3, 1958*, Cmnd. 859 (1959–60) XXXVI, pp. 2–4.

17. Bartlett, *The Long Retreat*, p. 109.

18. A. J. Pierre, *Nuclear Politics: The British Experience with an Independent Strategic Force, 1939–1970* (Oxford University Press, 1972) p. 316; J. Baylis, 'The Anglo-American Relationship in Defence', in J. Baylis (ed.), *British Defence Policy in the Changing World* (Croom Helm, 1977) pp. 85–6.

19. H. G. Nicholas, *The United States and Britain* (University of Chicago Press, 1974) p. 165; D. Nunnerley, *President Kennedy and Britain* (Bodley Head, 1972) pp. 129 and 158.

20. C. Bell, *The Debatable Alliance: an essay in Anglo-American relations* (Oxford University Press, 1964) p. 96.

21. *The Times* (4 Oct 1957) p. 4.

22. H. Kissinger, *The Necessity for Choice* (Chatto and Windus, 1960) p. 112; A. J. Pierre, *Nuclear Politics: the British Experience with an Independent Strategic Force, 1939–1970* (Oxford University Press, 1972) p. 316.

23. M. Camps, *Britain and the European Community 1955–1963* (Princeton University Press, 1964) p. 500; J. Newhouse, *De Gaulle and the Anglo-Saxons* (New York: Viking, 1970) pp. 211, 226–8; W. L. Kohl, *French Nuclear Diplomacy* (Princeton University Press, 1971) pp. 331–2.

24. J. Frankel, *British Foreign Policy 1945–1973* (Oxford University Press, 1975) pp. 234–8.

25. International Institute of Strategic Studies, *The Military Balance 1975–76* (1975) p. 73 and *The Military Balance 1977–78* (1977) p. 79.

26. R. N. Rosecrance, *Defence of the Realm: British Strategy in the Nuclear Epoch* (New York: Columbia University Press, 1968) pp. 154–64 and 184–5.

27. 'Nassau Communiqué' (21 Dec 1962), H. Macmillan, *At the End of the Day, 1961–1963* (Macmillan, 1973) app. 4, p. 555.

28. R. N. Rosecrance, *Defence of the Realm: British Strategy in the Nuclear Epoch* (New York: Columbia University Press, 1968) p. 17.

29. R. Cook and D. Smith, 'Buy a new H-Bomb – the easy way', *New Statesman* (12 Jan 1979) 43.

30. *Defence: Outline of Future Policy*, Cmnd. 124 (1956–7) XXIII, p. 3; and *Report on Defence 1960*, Cmnd. 952 (1959–60) XXIV, p. 5.

31. W. P. Snyder, *The Politics of British Defence Policy, 1945–1962* (Columbus: Ohio State University Press, 1964) p. 234. See also A. MacLaren, 'Britain's Strategic Nuclear Force', *Military Review*, LVII 3 (Mar 1977) 74.

32. US Congress, Senate Committee on Foreign Relations, *Briefings on SALT Negotiations*, 95th Congress, First Session (1977) p. 30.

33. *Twelfth Report of the Expenditure Committee*, Cmnd. 399 (1972–3) XXII, p. ix.

34. Air-Vice-Marshal S. W. B. Menaul, 'The Shifting Theater Nuclear Balance in Europe', *The Strategic Review*, VI 4 (Fall 1978) 34–45.

35. I. Smart, *The Future of the British Deterrent: Technical, Economic and Strategic Issues* (The Royal Institute of International Affairs, 1977) p. 13.

36. R. Cook and D. Smith, 'Buy a new H-Bomb – the easy way', *New Statesman* (12 Jan 1979) 43.

37. Chatham House Briefings, *Foreign Policy and the New Government*, no. 1 (The Royal Institute of International Affairs, 1979) p. 5.

38. J. J. Martin, 'Nuclear Weapons in NATO's Deterrent Strategy', *Orbis*, XXII, 4 (Winter 1979) 878–80.

39. C. Bell, *The Debatable Alliance: an essay in Anglo-American relations* (Oxford University Press, 1964) p. 126. See also A. J. Groom, 'The British Deterrent', in J. Baylis (ed.), *British Defence Policy in a Changing World* (Croom Helm, 1977) p. 143.

40. *The Times* (3 June 1976) p. 4.

41. E. Heath, *Old World, New Horizons: Britain, the Common Market and the Atlantic Alliance* (Oxford University Press, 1970) p. 73.

42. W. Joshua and W. F. Hahn, *Nuclear Politics: America, France and Britain*, The Washington Papers (Beverly Hills: Sage Publications, 1973) vol. I, 9, pp. 22–37.

43. I. Smart, 'Future Conditional: The Prospect for Anglo-French Nuclear Co-operation', *Adelphi Papers*, no. 78 (1971) p. 29.

44. J. Isnard, 'La place de l'Europe dans les negotiations SALT', *Le Monde* (4 Jan 1979) p. 1.

45. J. Bellini and G. Pattie, *A New World Role for the Medium Power: the British Opportunity* (Royal United Services Institute, 1977) p. 39.

46. Ibid., p. 42.

47. I. Smart, *The Future of the British Deterrent: Technical, Economic and Strategic Issues* (The Royal Institute of International Affairs, 1977) pp. 65–6.

48. *Aviation Week and Space Technology* (28 Mar 1977) p. 48.

49. Aviation Week and Space Technology, *Particle-Beam Weapon Development* (New York: McGraw Hill, 1978) pp. 11-12.

50. R. L. Garwin, 'Charged-Particle beam weapons?', *The Bulletin of Atomic Scientists*, XXXIV, 8 (Oct 1978) 24–7. See also J. Parmentola and K. Tsipis, 'Particle-Beam Weapons', *Scientific American*, CCXL, 4 (Apr 1979) 38–49.

List of Contributors

THE LATE LORD STRANG served in the Foreign Office from 1919 to 1953 (as head of the Central Department, 1937–9; British representative on the European Advisory Commission, 1943–5; Permanent Under-Secretary, 1949–53). He wrote *Britain in World Affairs* and *Home and Abroad*.

GRAHAM ROSS has taught international history and international relations at the University of Leeds since 1964. He is editing a collection of Foreign Office despatches, minutes and memoranda relating to policy towards the Soviet Union between 1941 and 1945.

PROFESSOR MARGARET GOWING holds the chair of the History of Science at the University of Oxford; she is the author of *Britain and Atomic Energy, 1939–45; Independence and Deterrence: Britain and Atomic Energy 1945–52* (2 vols) and of two volumes in the civil series of official histories of the Second World War: *British War Economy* (with Professor Sir Keith Hancock) and *Civil Industry and Trade* (with E. L. Hargreaves).

DR EDWARD SPIERS has been Defence Lecturer in the School of History at Leeds since 1975. He has written extensively about modern strategic issues; his other chief interest lies in the British army of the nineteenth century.

PROFESSOR SARVEPALLI GOPAL teaches at the Centre for Historical Studies, Jawaharlal Nehru University, Delhi. The third volume of his authorised biography of Nehru is expected in 1981.

PROFESSOR DAVID DILKS has held the chair of International History at the University of Leeds since 1970. He is engaged upon a biography of Neville Chamberlain.

Index